Assessment, Evaluation and Sex & Relationships Education

A practical guide for education, health and community settings

Second edition

Simon Blake and Stella Muttock

Revised by Sam Beal and Lisa Handy

The Sex Education Forum is the national authority on sex and relationships education (SRE). It is a unique collaboration of over 90 member organisations and 750 practitioners with representatives from health, education, faith, disability and children's organisations. We believe that all children and young people have the right to good SRE and aim to provide all professionals involved in SRE with the information they need to ensure this right.

If you work with young people, in school or in a youth or community setting as a teacher, health professional, social worker or you are a parent or carer we can help provide you with the information and support you need to provide effective sex and relationships education. We work with teachers and health professionals across all settings promoting good practice through a range of publications and factsheets. If you have a query or need more information about any aspect of SRE you can e-mail us at sexedforum@ncb.org.uk or visit www.ncb.org.uk/sef.

NCB's vision is a society in which children and young people contribute, are valued and their rights respected. NCB aims to:

- reduce inequalities of opportunity in childhood
- ensure children and young people can use their voice to improve their lives and the lives of those around them
- improve perceptions of children and young people
- enhance the health, learning, experiences and opportunities of children and young people
- encourage the building of positive and supportive relationships for children and young people with families, carers, friends and communities
- provide leadership through the use of evidence and research to improve policy and practice.

NCB has adopted and works within the UN Convention on the Rights of the Child.

Published by NCB

NCB, 8 Wakley Street, London EC1V 7QE
Tel: 0207 843 6000
Website: www.ncb.org.uk
Registered charity number: 258825

NCB works in partnership with Children in Scotland (www.childreninscotland.org.uk) and Children in Wales (www.childreninwales.org.uk).

ISBN: 978 1 907969 50 8
Ebook ISBN: 978 1 907969 70 6

Second edition
First edition published 2004

British Library Cataloguing in Publication Data
A catalogue record for this book is available from the British Library

The views expressed in this book are those of the authors and not necessarily those of NCB.
All photos are posed by models.

Typeset by Saxon Graphics Limited, Derby
Printed by Hobbs the Printers Limited, Brunel Road, Totton

Contents

Acknowledgements

First edition

This toolkit was written by Simon Blake and Stella Muttock and in collaboration with children, young people and workers from schools and community settings across Camden and Islington who talked to the original authors about learning and assessment, to who we give our thanks.

Thank you to the members of the advisory group: Joy Ashwin, Shirley Blenman, Helen Cameron, Simon Forrest, Steve Gray, Gill Morris, Tanya Procter, Jamie Smith, Karen Sparkes, Verena Thompson and Susan Thorp.

Thank you to Anna Martinez, Vanessa Cooper and Gill Frances for their ideas, contributions and comments on earlier drafts.

Many of the structures and approaches will be familiar to those experienced in group work and active learning methods, assessment and evaluation tools. Thank you to colleagues whose creativity and ideas have (often unknown to them) inspired materials in this toolkit.

Thank you again to Helen Cameron and Tanya Procter, this time for commissioning the toolkit and for their support throughout, as well as the following agencies:

- Camden and Islington Healthy School Scheme
- Camden and Islington Teenage Pregnancy Team
- Camden Local Education Authority
- CEA@Islington

Second edition

The second edition of this toolkit has also been a collaborative effort. We would like to thank everyone who was involved. We would like to pay particular thanks to Sam Beal, who played a big part in updating this resource.

The National Children's Bureau is also grateful for the advice on assessment provided by Dr John Lloyd, and thanks Philippa Hoyle, who contributed many ideas and resources to this revised version. Thanks also goes to Anna Martinez and Fergus Crow for their ideas, contributions, and comments on earlier drafts.

Sam Beal
Partnership Adviser - Health and Wellbeing, Healthy Schools Team, Brighton & Hove

The Healthy Schools Team works in collaboration with partners in health, the community and voluntary sector and schools to provide effective consultancy support and training in primary, secondary and special schools to develop PSHE, Healthy Schools, anti-bullying and equalities practice. The Healthy Schools Team has a history of developing innovative curriculum materials and guidance to support the development of the PSHE curriculum.

Dr John Lloyd
Policy Adviser at the PSHE Association. John was formerly an adviser for PSHE and Citizenship at the DCSF.

The PSHE Association is the subject association for all professionals working in Personal, Social, Health and Economic education. Its mission is to raise the status, quality and impact of PSHEe, and enable high quality teaching and learning in schools.

Philippa Hoyle
Teaching and Learning Consultant, Pupil Wellbeing and Vulnerable Learners, Standards Learning and Effectiveness Service (SLES), East Sussex County Council

The Pupil Wellbeing and Vulnerable Learners team have a long history of working to support all schools in East Sussex in addressing and raising the profile of health and wellbeing issues for young people through the provision of advice, support, training for schools, staff, young people and governors as well as developing a range of guidance materials and support services to schools working in partnership with the primary care trust.

Lisa Handy
Acting Principal Officer: SRE and Sexual Health
Sex Education Forum
National Children's Bureau
March 2012

Preface to second edition

Good SRE equips children and young people with the skills and confidence to manage their lives as they move through puberty and adolescence into adulthood. SRE needs to support all children and young people – especially those who are most vulnerable or excluded – in accessing relevant information, developing emotional and social skills, and clarifying beliefs and values about sex and relationships.

Assessment and evaluation play a key role in the development of effective SRE. Yet both are currently underdeveloped in everyday practice in both schools and community work. This has been highlighted in both the 2007 and 2010 Ofsted PSHE Education reports; identifying assessment as the weakest aspect of PSHE Education teaching. Ofsted reports highlight that some schools believe pupil's enjoyment of the subject is due in part to the absence of an assessment framework, however in recent years this attitude has started to change and examples of good practice have been identified.

This edition is designed to support this change in attitudes by being a much more school focused resource but with exercises that non-school practitioners will still find useful in improving practice.

During the consultation of the sector, carried out by the Sex Education Forum to feed into the 2011 review of PSHE Education, it became apparent that many practitioners often interchange the two processes of evaluation and assessment. Therefore, to help clarify the difference between the two, this edition has split the assessment and evaluation activities into separate sections. Pages 10 and 11 help explain why they are different, while sections 3 and 4 list some new and revised activities and their methods of use in more detail. The assessment activities include a suggestion of what type of assessment it best serves, e.g. before a programme starts, to inform the facilitator what the learner/s need (needs assessment), during a programme to inform the facilitator how well the learner/s are doing (summative) or at the end of a programme to see what the learner/s have learnt (formative). The evaluation activities have also been split to identify whether they are better used during a programme or after (summative or formative).

Introduction

Sex and relationships education (SRE) is learning about the emotional, social and physical aspects of growing up, relationships, sex, human sexuality and sexual health. It should equip children and young people with the information, skills and values to have safe, fulfilling and enjoyable relationships and to take responsibility for their sexual health and well-being. (SEF, 2012)

Assessment and evaluation play a key role in the effective teaching and learning of SRE within Personal, Social, Health and Economic (PSHE) Education. The PSHE Association comments on the importance of assessment to PSHE education:

> Assessment is as important in PSHE education as in every other curriculum area and for the same reasons: young people have a right to know how they are doing in every subject; teachers need to know how pupils are progressing, in order to inform future teaching and learning; the school leadership team, parents, governors and, of course, Ofsted inspectors need to see the impact PSHE education is having for young people and the part it is playing for the school in achieving the three statutory aims of the National Curriculum ... (and meeting) higher grade descriptors of the ... Ofsted framework. If we do not assess learning, then all we can do is *describe* what we do in PSHE education but not what impact it has.
>
> *PSHE Association,* 2011

Assessment is a process through which judgements are made about an individual's learning and development. Evaluation is a process through which judgements are made about how effectively particular teaching approaches, activities and materials meet specific learning objectives.

Children and young people will also need to be made aware of the changes that have been made as a result of the evaluation they have been involved in, so that they know that their contribution has been worthwhile. Some of the activities described include reflective questions to inform evaluation.

Are you getting it right? A toolkit for consulting young people on sex and relationships education (SEF, 2008) provides a selection of activities to help secondary schools involve young people when reviewing and auditing their SRE with the purpose of ensuring that provision meets their needs. The toolkit promotes discussion with children and young people about how SRE should be taught, and what should be covered. The activities contained within it provide complementary ideas for how SRE can be evaluated.

Evidence shows that both processes are important in securing pupil progress and achievement. The 2012 Ofsted Evaluation Schedule includes a focus on the use of assessment to support effective learning and will prioritise pupil achievement.

*"Teaching should be understood to include teachers' planning and implementing of learning activities across the whole curriculum, as well as marking, assessment and feedback. ...The judgement on the quality of teaching **must take account of evidence of pupils' learning and progress**" (Ofsted 2012)*

Many schools and community settings have worked hard to develop systems and expertise in assessing and evaluating SRE; however, for a variety of reasons, evaluation and in particular assessment remain underdeveloped. For example, the Ofsted Report Personal, Social, Health and Economic Education in Schools (2010) found the following:

The assessment and tracking of pupils' progress in PSHE education were inadequate in 15 of the 73 secondary schools visited. The assessment of PSHE was ineffective in important respects in about half of the primary and secondary schools, although elements of it were in place.

Teachers could give feedback to learners to let them know what to do better next time.
(Year 7 boy, in a secondary school talking about the best way to be assessed in PSHE Education.)

Local authorities such as Camden Education Authority, CEA@Islington, Brighton & Hove City Council and East Sussex County Council have a strong history of working to ensure that assessment is core to good teaching and learning.

This toolkit builds on work done in these local authorities and by the PSHE Association. The toolkit was originally developed following a review of the literature and existing resources, advice and guidance; and after extensive consultation with children, young people and practitioners. It has since been revised to reflect some of the changes in policy and offers practical advice, guidance and activities for workers across different settings on the why, what and how of assessment and evaluation in SRE.

This toolkit is based on a belief that learning in SRE is most effective when we:

- establish what children and young people already know and set relevant success criteria and goals with them
- ensure that children and young people actively participate in the learning process
- work with children and young people to ensure they make progress in their learning and can reflect on the progress made
- clarify future learning needs
- celebrate progress and achievement
- routinely identify and reflect upon how effective our practice is and how to improve it to best meet the needs of the children and young people we work with.

For this edition, the resource has been divided into four sections. Section 1 gives a brief overview of best practice in SRE. Section 2 summarises the theory and practice of assessment and evaluation. Section 3 offers a comprehensive range of practical activities for assessing learning and Section 4 offers a wide range of practical activities for evaluating practice.

Children, young people and the importance of sex and relationships education

1

Children, young people and the importance of sex and relationships education

Children and young people learn about sex and relationships both formally and informally. Formal learning happens as a result of planned opportunities with parents, peers, carers, learning mentors, health workers, teachers and youth workers, as well as from leaflets, books and websites. Children and young people also learn informally from the media – including soap operas, television programmes and films – and from both negative and positive situations going on around them – for example, if their parents divorce or separate, if there is domestic violence, or if there are positive and happy relationships with family and friends. Some of what children and young people learn is accurate and helpful; some of it is based on misinformation, ignorance and prejudice, and can leave children and young people unprepared for the physical and emotional changes involved in growing up and the many cultural and societal challenges of the 21st century world.

The prevailing culture within Britain is one in which we do not always talk sensibly about sex and relationships. Myths and misconceptions abound. Stereotypes and prejudices, for example about sexuality, teenage parenthood and people living with HIV, can be reinforced and perpetuated at home, at school and in the media. Sexual imagery is prevalent in the media and advertising. This culture can lead to silence, embarrassment and misinformation about sex, sexuality and relationships. While there have been improvements in the information, advice and support that we provide for young people on sex and relationships, due to the implementation of the Teenage Pregnancy Strategy between 1998 and 2008, there is still some way to go. Young people themselves report gaps in their knowledge. For example, in a recent survey carried about by the Sex Education Forum (2011) nearly half (49 per cent) of young people said they had not learnt all they needed to know about HIV and AIDS.

Children and young people need to grow up with the knowledge and understanding that helps them to understand their body and how it changes, as well as knowing about sex, sexuality, relationships and sexual health. They also need planned opportunities to develop the skills they need so they can move confidently and safely through puberty into adolescence and adulthood. The effective assessment and evaluation of SRE is a key ingredient in ensuring that programmes delivered meet the needs of children and young people.

The Sex Education Forum believes that quality SRE should:

- Be accurate and factual, covering a comprehensive range of information about sex, relationships, the law and sexual health, in order to make informed choices. In schools this should be part of compulsory curriculum provision.
- Be positively inclusive in terms of gender, sexual orientation, disability, ethnicity, culture, age, religion or belief or other life-experience particularly HIV status and pregnancy.
- Include the development of skills to support healthy and safe relationships and ensure good communication about these issues.

- Promote a critical awareness of the different attitudes and views on sex and relationships within society such as peer norms and those portrayed in the media.
- Provide opportunities for reflection in order to nurture personal values based on mutual respect and care.
- Be part of lifelong learning, starting early in childhood and continuing throughout life. It should reflect the age and level of the pupil.
- Ensure children and young people are clearly informed of their rights such as how they can access confidential advice and health services within the boundaries of safeguarding.
- Be relevant and meet the needs of children and young people, and actively involve them as participants, advocates and evaluators in developing good quality provision.
- Be delivered by competent and confident educators.
- Be provided within a learning environment that is safe for the children, young people and adults involved and based on the principle that prejudice, discrimination and bullying are harmful and unacceptable.

(SEF, 2012)

Throughout the development of the original version of this toolkit, children and young people stressed the importance of adults taking SRE seriously so that they get the quality of education and support that they want. Effective assessment can contribute to the valuing of SRE by workers, senior managers and pupils.

As one nine-year-old said: 'Because there are not exams, they are not worried and let you mess around.'

Terminology

Professionals in different settings use different language and approaches when working with children and young people on sex and relationships. In this toolkit, we use the term sex and relationships education (SRE) to mean planned opportunities to develop pupil knowledge and skills and to enable them to explore and clarify values and attitudes. Table 1.1: Approaches to SRE (page 6) illustrates how the approach and methodologies may differ and clarifies that the overall process is the same across settings and professional disciplines.

Table 1.1 Approaches to SRE

	School and further education
Step 1: **Identifying need**	• Formal review of the PSHE and Citizenship curriculum or local healthy schools audit • Findings from pupil surveys, questionnaires, school council, class discussions, private suggestion boxes • Local trends in health issues, e.g. increase in chlamydia • Findings from school health profile • Results from national and local research projects • Evaluation of previous units/modules • Minimum standards suggested by local authority • Local authority SRE policy • Parental needs and expectations • School governors' expectations
Step 2: **Responding to need**	• Curriculum review, SRE/senior management team with pupil input • Development of new lesson plans, PSHE and Citizenship coordinator • Identification of new resources • Identification of outside agencies and visitors • Identification of professional development needs • Consultations with pupils, parents and carers • Peer training
Step 3: **Delivering SRE**	• SRE teacher team • Tutors • Class teachers • Peer groups • School nurses • Outside agencies and visitors
Step 4: **Assessment of pupil learning as an ongoing process (see Figure 2.2)**	• Self-assessment • Peer assessment, role-plays, group reviews, circle time • Informal teacher assessment, observations, questioning • Formal teacher assessment, quizzes, work samples
Step 5: **Evaluation of teaching programme**	• Range of techniques and activities • Views from pupils, visitors and teachers • Peer education reviews • Formal independent reviews
Step 6: **Reporting and recording progress**	• Marking • Parent/carer consultation • Samples collected for portfolio • School systems for PSHE and Citizenship • Celebratory displays, assemblies, presentations, activities

Youth, community and secure settings	One-to-one work, including health services, youth offending teams and social care
• National and local trends and research • Young people's responses during consultation • Local health profiling	• Individual care plan • Directly from the child/young person in response to events • Based on personal history • Results from local and national research and trends • Consultations with health professionals, learning mentors, practice nurses, carers, social workers, youth offending team workers • Screening
• Consultations with children and young people by individual youth workers and teams and parents/carers • Advice and support from external agencies • Peer training	• Consultations with child or young person • Consultations with relevant workers • Advice and support • Screening
• One-to-one input with external support from relevant agencies and personnel • Small-group input, with youth worker(s) as facilitators or personnel from external agencies • Peer groups	• One-to-one input with external support from relevant agencies and personnel
• Self-assessment • Peer assessment • Checking understanding with child/ young person/group	• Checking with child or young person that they understand • Finding out what else they need
• Personal or group review to determine what was helpful and unhelpful • Formal and informal evaluating activities • Peer education reviews • Formal independent reviews	• Asking child or young person whether they understand • Formal independent reviews
• Personal portfolios • Local education authority's monitoring and inspections	• Individual care plans

2

Assessment and evaluation

Assessment and evaluation

This section begins with definitions of *assessment, recording of learning, evaluation* and *monitoring.* It then goes on to provide more detailed information about assessment and evaluation. The activities in Sections 3 and 4 provide a range of assessment and evaluation tools that can be used as they are or adapted to suit a particular group or setting. Good practice in the assessment, evaluation and monitoring of SRE will mirror that in other areas of the curriculum; whether that curriculum is provided in schools or through a youth setting.

Definitions

Assessment

"Assessment is an essential and integral part of effective teaching and learning in all subjects including PSHE education. It checks that learning is taking place and shows what learners can do well, and where and how they can do better. It allows progress to be recognised and celebrated and it informs the next steps and priorities of both teachers and learners."

(PSHE Association, 2010)

Assessment in SRE as part of PSHE education is not about making judgements about the character, worth or values of individual pupils nor is it about continual testing. It is the same as in any other subject, an integral part of learning. It describes a range of activities that includes:

- informing the learning process through identifying needs (assessment for learning)
- completing the learning cycle effectively by providing opportunities to reflect upon what has been learnt and how it can be put into action, thus having the potential to support progress and affect behaviour (assessment for learning)
- collecting information to certify achievement and competence (assessment of learning) and to inform others (assessment of learning).

Assessment is not the sole responsibility of any one individual. A range of people – including peers, youth workers, learning mentors, teachers, and other community partners – can carry out assessment. Those working in a 1:1 situation have a particularly important role to play in working with vulnerable and marginalised children and young people. For example, appropriately trained staff may conduct screening sessions with teenagers to assess the level of sexual health risk-taking behaviour and to develop appropriate learning opportunities, interventions and support as needed.

Do a before and after.
Young man, aged 13

Recording of learning

Learning is recorded for a number of reasons, such as illustrating the progress made by individual children and young people in PSHE Education and this has become more important now Ofsted has highlighted this in its guidance when carrying out section five inspections.

Many of the activities in section 3 can be used as evidence of learning for formal processes, including individual education plans, accreditation, reporting to parents and carers, meeting school-determined outcomes as part of the Healthy Schools Programme and school self-evaluation. By carrying out baseline and formative assessment with each child and young person, progress can be evidenced using the same school (or setting) systems used for other curriculum subjects and topics, helping to illustrate the effectiveness of the SRE programme or intervention.

Evaluation

Evaluation is concerned with finding out how effective activities, materials and approaches have been in achieving the aims and objectives of a learning experience and their impact on the target audience. Evaluating SRE provides valuable knowledge and insight for the worker to use so that, as future work evolves and develops, effectiveness is improved.

Monitoring

Monitoring is about keeping track of implementation when a project or agreed activity is in progress. It ensures that activities and materials are being used according to the policy and relate to previously agreed objectives. In schools this might include the PSHE Coordinator checking that the SRE programme is being delivered through; work scrutinies, lesson observations and pupil feedback.

Assessment – why, what and how?

Why is assessment important?
Assessment is important because it:

- enables everyone to know what has been learnt, secures motivation and commitment, and supports self-esteem and emotional and social development
- helps to make learning real for children and young people and potentially helps to influence or change behaviour
- identifies what else needs to be learnt in the future
- enables everyone to recognise, record and report on progress across all areas of emotional and social development, hence encouraging recognition and celebration. It also contributes to success in meeting individual goals and plans, such as personal education plans
- helps to raise the status of work on SRE amongst children, young people, their families, teachers and other professionals
- develops skills of reflection and feedback in children and young people and so supports their emotional and social development
- provides evidence, where relevant, of the impact of SRE for healthy schools, school self-evaluation, commissioners of pieces of work, quality assurance and formal accreditation processes such as ASDAN (Award Scheme Development and Accreditation Network) and NOCN (National Open College Network).

Black and William (1998) believe that improving learning through assessment depends on:

- providing effective feedback to children and young people
- actively involving children and young people in their own learning
- adjusting teaching to take account of the results of assessment
- recognising the profound influence that assessment has on the motivation and self-esteem of children and young people, both of which are crucial influences on learning
- children and young people learning how to assess themselves and understanding how to improve.

What are the different types of assessment?
There are a number of different types of assessment that are carried out, each with a different purpose in mind. Assessment is used both to assess what has been learnt and what needs to be learnt. The key types of assessment are: baseline, formative and summative.

Baseline assessment
Baseline or needs assessment (assessment for learning) is carried out at the beginning of a piece of work for three specific purposes:

- to determine what is already known
- to clarify learning needs
- to identify whether children or young people have any special educational needs (if not already known).

Practitioners can do a baseline assessment to determine where to start, and to guide them in how the work should be developed, including what language and resources to use.

One quick and effective baseline assessment method is a brainstorm or the use of graffiti sheets. For example, at the start of a planned piece of work, ask children and young people to write down their ideas in response to various statements 'Everything we know about.HIV ... ', 'Everything we think we know about HIV ... ' 'What we'd like to know about HIV ... ' The list can then be used to plan or amend the content and learning objectives collaboratively to meet the needs of the individual or group. For younger children, 'draw and write' activities provide a useful baseline assessment method. (Please see examples in Section 3.)

More detailed information about how assessment for learning can promote learning and raise standards of learning is available from http://www.aaia.org.uk/afl/assessment-reform-group/

Formative assessment
Formative assessment is also assessment for learning and occurs when workers, children and young people work together to make judgements about progress being made against agreed learning objectives. This is then used to identify the next teaching/learning steps. It is a dynamic, collaborative process that enhances the learning experience.

Therefore an ongoing process of assessment should occur continuously alongside a programme with everyone considering, either individually or in a group, the impact of the learning on them. Often, information gained through observing the process is not discussed with children and young people openly and opportunities for learning are lost.

Formative assessment involves both reviewing and reflecting on progress and therefore involves the child's ability to engage in self and peer assessment – to reflect on and analyse personal responses to the work. This is a skill for everyday living that will need to be taught and developed alongside the assessment process. For example; the Social and Emotional Aspects of Learning (SEAL) materials[1] can be used to develop the skills of self-awareness, giving constructive feedback and using appropriate listening and discussion skills.

Assessing a sample of the work produced by pupils can be done throughout the year to monitor and provide evidence of progress being made.

Summative assessment

Summative assessment (assessment of learning) is carried out at the end of a period of time or a piece of work. Progress and achievement is judged in relation to a set of criteria. These criteria or outcomes may be identified in a variety of documents such as personal education plans (PEPS), End of Key Stage Statements or action plans. Some of these sets of criteria are available locally or nationally as benchmarks for assessing progress, others may be developed by children and young people with a key worker such as a learning mentor, youth worker or social worker.

The results of the assessment are used to provide quantitative evidence for reporting to parents, teachers and other professionals and celebrating achievement with pupils. Summative assessment can also be used to develop future learning goals.

Summative assessments can involve tests, exams and written work, but do not have to do so. For example, group work can be used to assess communication skills, role-plays can be used to assess negotiation and risk management skills.

How is assessment carried out?

In order to be able to assess learning effectively, workers need to be clear about the learning objectives being worked towards. This in turn requires a planned programme that identifies learning objectives and learning outcomes and the activities and resources that will be used to meet these objectives. Planning in schools will be informed by National Curriculum programmes of study and national and local guidance.

A learning objective is what the pupils are going to learn expressed in terms of skills to be learned and developed, knowledge and understanding to be gained and values and attitudes to be considered. This is distinct from a description of what activities or tasks the pupils will do or what topic they are learning about.

---

1 At the time of publication SEAL materials are available from www.teachfind.com

We might use the following language when explaining objectives to pupils:

- Know that …
- Understand how/why …
- Develop/be able to …
- Be aware of …
- Explore/refine strategies for …[2]

The learning outcome is what you measure when you assess. The learning outcome is what pupils will do/say/write in the lesson that demonstrates they have reached the learning objective. Learning outcomes should be identified within the context of the actual lesson being taught.

For example

Learning objective
To understand the physical and emotional changes that take place at puberty
(3f PSHE: Personal Wellbeing: Programme of Study, National Curriculum 2007)

Intended learning outcomes

- Working towards: I can list two physical changes and three emotional changes at puberty.
- Working at: I can list a range of physical and emotional changes in both boys and girls.
- Working beyond: I can explain the physical and emotional changes that take place as a normal part of growing up and explain how these can impact on our identity and self-image

---

Best practice would involve practitioners working with pupils to identify the success criteria for the activity or piece of learning.

The method of assessment chosen needs to be fit for purpose and appropriate to the learning to ensure that the activity does actually assess the learning set out in the outcome. A single learning objective matched by learning outcomes is sufficient for a focused assessment activity.

Workers can generally use the teaching and learning activities they are using in lessons to assess learning, but this does not mean that every activity needs to be assessed. Workers should identify those activities that will show progress towards the goal. Teachers will generally use the National Curriculum End of Key Stage Statements to assess progress against.

---

2 DfES (2004): *Pedagogy and Practice – Assessment for Learning*

People need to know what HIV is and what happens if you have HIV – you have to work out how you will know they have learnt about it without scaring them.
Young man, aged 15

Case study

PSHE Association Progression Frameworks for Planning & Assessment
QCDA has published 'End of Key Stage Statements' for PSHE education that indicate pupils' expected attainment at the end of each Key Stage and many schools use these to identify whether a pupil is working towards, at or beyond. But where PSHE education differs from most other subjects, is that there are no National Curriculum levels against which to assess progress on a week-by-week, or term-by-term basis and through which to ensure progression when planning a programme, or series of lessons. To support (secondary) PSHE education coordinators and teachers in this, the PSHE Association have developed two frameworks for secondary settings (one for 'Personal wellbeing' and one for 'Economic wellbeing and financial capability') that take the 'key concepts' from the National Curriculum programmes of study and break each sub-section down into three broad 'level descriptors'.

Please see an extract from the *Personal Wellbeing Progression Framework*, Concept 1.2 Healthy Lifestyles (PSHE Association, 2010) on page 14.

Assessing learning in SRE

Effective sex and relationships education involves the development of knowledge and understanding, skills and opportunities to explore and clarify attitudes and values. Different types of assessment may be needed to assess progress in these different areas of learning. The activity chosen should be fit for purpose.

Assessing knowledge and understanding
Assessment of knowledge and understanding can be applied in the normal running of lessons or sessions through activities such as quizzes, and written work such as responding to letters and scenarios. It is important to use a variety of methods, ensuring that not all are based on writing.

Assessing attitudes and values
The assessment of pupil attitudes and values is not appropriate as this would involve inappropriate judgements about individuals. However, it would be appropriate to assess the ability or skills of a pupil to participate in activities related to exploring their attitudes and those of others.

Assessing skill development and the ability to explore values and attitudes
Skill development and an ability to explore values and attitudes can be demonstrated in a number of ways, including carrying out research, preparing presentations, writing a diary, and taking part in a group discussion or debate. Setting scenarios and role-playing are particularly useful because they are multi-purpose: they can be used to provide evidence of skills and levels of understanding.

Approaches to assessment

Reflection
The learning cycle in Figure 2.1 is a reminder of the importance of reflection in the learning process.

Figure 2.1 The learning cycle

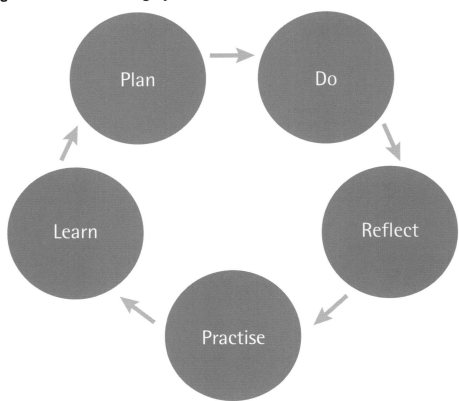

The following are examples of questions that can be used with pupils to support the reflection stage and to develop pupil understanding of what they have learned and the progress they have made:

- What new information have I learnt?
- What do I now think and believe?
- Has listening to the views of others changed my views and/or beliefs?
- Did it help me confirm what I really believe?
- Did I learn anything I did not expect to?
- How will it change my behaviour in the future?
- What do I know already?
- How did I feel about what I found out?
- What feelings did I have during the session?
- What do I now need to learn?
- Is there anyone else I need to talk to about this?

Individual responses could be recorded in a logbook or a diary.

Self-assessment and peer assessment
Self-assessment is when a child or young person asks himself or herself, or is asked, to assess their progress towards the learning objective and learning outcomes.

Peer assessment involves peers making a judgement about the knowledge, understanding, skills and confidence of their peers. It is vital that a safe learning environment is created before this method of assessment is used in order to avoid any potential embarrassment and hurtful comments. Children and young people will need to learn how to offer constructive feedback.

If peer and self-assessment are to be conducted properly pupils will need to be clear about what the learning objective and learning outcome is and what might count as evidence of the learning.

Case study

Self-assessment in SRE

In the academic year 2010–2011 Chester Schools' Christian Work (CSCW) funded by ACET, a Christian organisation, instigated a new monitoring and evaluation system that aims to record the impact of each one-hour session. At the beginning and end of each session the young people are anonymously polled on two questions, the responses to which record the impact the lesson has had on two specific issues.

The polling is done by simply asking the young person to close their eyes and put their hand in the air making a fist, a statement is read out and if the students agree they are asked to open their hand wide. The sessions start with a few warm-up statements and then finish with two statements that directly relate to the aims of that session. This short two-minute exercise is employed at the start and finish of each session. The SRE worker writes down the number of students in the class and the number of students who agree at the start and the end on a standard report form. The forms are used by all our workers and are collected to provide statistics for reporting on the impact of our work.

The statements for each lesson are standardised across all work CSCW do in one year. Each session will use statements that attempt to assess change in attitude and increases in knowledge. The statements are meant to be specific and measurable. For example, we would not ask 'What have you learnt about STIs?' but instead ask 'Can you name three STIs?' to specifically track if their knowledge has increased. Our second question for the sexually transmitted infection session is about how confidence in staying safe has changed. This attempts to monitor what impact our session has had on attitudes.

CSCW have found this exercise a very achievable method of directly monitoring SRE sessions. It is quick enough and easy enough that all workers can be easily trained to employ it and it does not take so much time that it impinges on the core business of providing education. They are continuing to use this method in their work this academic year but are also looking to employ other methods to track long term more detailed results.

Structured informal assessment

This is when the facilitator makes planned observations of individuals or groups as they work. The young people are observed against clearly identified criteria and questions, to help check the learning. Children and young people should be aware that this type of assessment of their personal learning is ongoing, and they should know and understand when and how to expect feedback.

Observations done in this way are particularly useful for assessing:

- the quality of collaboration, and abilities such as listening to others, turn-taking, and respecting the views of others
- the different or preferred roles that individuals take on in groups during a set task, for example, making decisions, keeping the group on task, having good ideas, leading the group
- the development of skills such as team working.

Structured formal assessment

Formal assessments are normally made when progress is being recorded. They are normally carried out in relation to set (often national) targets to see if a certain standard or level has been reached. This often takes the form of a written test or a portfolio of evidence. Exam boards such as Award Scheme Development and Accreditation Network (ASDAN) and the National Open College Network (NOCN) can provide accredited SRE courses that can contribute to the qualifications held by young people.

Using evidence of learning

Many of the assessment activities covered in Section 3 generate a range of material that provides evidence of learning and achievement. This material can be helpfully used, both formally and informally, to:

- provide feedback/reports to children, young people and their families
- provide evidence of the impact of the programme for school senior leadership teams, Ofsted and funders
- identify whether there are individuals or groups of children and young people who may need additional support
- identify future learning needs so as to inform planning and multi-agency working
- celebrate success and in doing so value individuals and raise self-esteem.

Figure 2.2 Different approaches to assessment

Assessment for learning

Private reflection	Regular entries in personal reflective diary
Self-assessment	Directed consideration of diary entries, group work activities
Peer assessment (within group)	Exchange of views between peers within a group or class
Peer assessment (with other groups)	Assessment takes place through exchanging views with another group, e.g. other classes, other schools, youth groups, older students
Structured informal assessment by worker	Ongoing observations, questioning, feedback to pupils
Structured formal assessment by worker	Quizzes, questionnaires, work samples Marked work for portfolios Internal tests
External examinations	Formal accreditation, Duke of Edinburgh Awards, Award Scheme and Accreditation Network (ASDAN), National Open College Network (NOCN)

Assessment of learning

Evaluation – why, what and how?

Why is evaluation important?

Evaluation helps us to reflect on planning and to receive feedback about what worked well and not so well. Hence it helps us to continually improve our provision for the children and young people we work with. Evaluating individual activities or the level of engagement of different members of the group, and using this to inform future planning, gives opportunities to amend our practice and, if necessary, refocus our objectives in the light of findings. Therefore, it contributes to ensuring the SRE we deliver has a positive impact on the learning of children and young people.

What are the different types of evaluation?

Evaluation is concerned with both impact and process.

Impact evaluation

Impact evaluation focuses on long-term outcomes and aims to identify the impact of a specific piece of work. Such evaluations are primarily concerned with identifying and measuring short, medium and long-term changes in attitudes and behaviour that can be attributed to the programme. As such, this type of evaluation demands high levels of technical expertise, resources and a lengthy time span.

Process evaluation

Process evaluation focuses on how a programme or a particular piece of work has been delivered and will be the type most commonly used in SRE. It uses reflection and feedback on the process of learning to inform immediate responses to situations and future planning. Most 'everyday' evaluation activities, including customer satisfaction surveys and feedback from training participants, focus on process issues. Process evaluations seek to answer questions such as:

- How well did the content of the programme address the needs of the group and or meet the learning objective and outcomes?
- To what extent was the programme accessible to the target group?
- What worked well, and what went less well (and why)?
- How could the learning be improved?

Evaluating the processes could involve:

- noting how everyone worked together
- reflecting on who kept on task and for how long
- reflecting on whether everyone was able to participate and achieve at their own level
- considering how activities were organised and delivered
- considering whether resources were fit for their purpose
- identifying what went well and what might be done differently next time.

How is evaluation carried out?

There are many different evaluation methods and these could involve observation, questionnaires and focus groups for example. Evaluation involves asking children and young people explicitly about the process of learning, for example asking them to judge whether an activity was useful, if the activity or grouping supported them in working well together, or

They should try and find out what we enjoyed and found interesting, and what they need to change.
Young woman, aged 17

I want to tell the teacher what they did well.
Girl, aged 9

whether the teaching enabled children and young people to access the intended learning. Asking about pupils' enjoyment of sessions may sometimes be useful, but practitioners should ask additionally about whether they were supported and challenged to learn.

Are you getting it right? A toolkit for consulting young people on sex and relationships education (SEF, 2008) provides examples of activities that can be used to review and evaluate a sex and relationship education programme.

Assessment of learning will of course contribute to the overall evaluation by enabling workers to identify whether the methods used, the environment and the approach were successful in achieving the learning objectives. Workers can also evaluate – by means of private reflection or by working with their colleagues to reflect and identify what has been achieved – and thereby inform future planning.

The questions in Figure 2.3 can be used to support a practitioner to reflect on a session they have just delivered. In addition it could be helpful in a peer review with a colleague or in supervision. At its best, evaluation combines input from children and young people with that of the workers.

Figure 2.3 Questions to consider either in supervision with a colleague or on your own

How do I feel at the end of the session?
What are my thoughts at the end of the session?
What was my overall impression of how well the session went?
What did I do well?
Were the participants involved and engaged?
Have the learning objectives been achieved?
How well did I work with the teaching assistant/other youth workers etc.?
What feedback have I received?
If I was to deliver this session again, what might I do differently in terms of: • Objectives? • Activities used? • Resources used? • Pace?
Do I have any personal and professional development needs?

Assessment activities

Assessment activities

Good practice involves checking pupils' progress regularly in PSHE education, just as teachers do for other subjects, with assessment taking place alongside all other work, using a wide range of assessment techniques and assessment evidence.

"In one of the primary schools visited, pupils had PSHE exercise books, completed tasks that were carefully marked and sat end of unit tests to identify if they were making progress. Points for improvement were provided and these allowed pupils to discuss their work with the teacher. The teachers were aware of the standards that pupils were working towards; these were linked to the end of key stage statements as well as to the PSHE framework. Self-assessment and peer assessment, such as commenting on each other's role-play or presentations, were used well, but they did not take the place of teacher assessment. The pupils' own comments and evaluations enabled teachers to follow up specific points and support individuals to develop strategies to overcome difficulties".

(Ofsted, 2010, P.20)

Assessment is a process through which 'judgements' are made about an individual's learning and development. In this section you will find a variety of activities that can be used to assess learning. The activities described can be used in a wide variety of ways. However, it is crucial that the activity is fit for purpose and is differentiated so that it can be accessed by all group members.

In order to assess the learning and progress being made you will find that some of the activities are linked to assessment frameworks provided by The QCDA/National Curriculum End of Key Stage Statements[3] and the PSHE Association Example Framework (2010) to illustrate how an activity can be used to assess learning against outcomes.

The activities are organised under three headings, as described below, although in some cases the activities can be used to assess in a variety of ways, with most being suitable for use both individually and in groups:

- baseline assessment (assessment for learning)
- formative assessment (assessment for learning)
- summative assessment (assessment of learning).

Supplementary assessment activities, originally published in the first edition of this book, are available at www.ncb.org.uk/resources/publications/support-resources/assessment-evaluation-and-sex-relationships-education

---

3 At the time of publication The QCDA / National Curriculum End of Key Stage Statements are available from www.teachfind.com

Summary of Assessment Activities

ASSESSMENT	Page	Baseline	Formative	Summative	Individually	Group
Advising others	49			✓	✓	✓
Carousel interviews	34		✓			✓
Diamond fours/nines	43		✓		✓	✓
Draw and write	26/60	✓		✓	✓	✓
Graffiti sheets	29	✓			✓	✓
My toolbox	47		✓		✓	✓
Peer assessment	41		✓			✓
Quizzes	66	✓	✓	✓	✓	✓
Role-play	51			✓		✓
Self-assessment	39		✓		✓	✓
Storyboards	61			✓	✓	✓
Sentence stems	37		✓		✓	✓
The story so far	38		✓		✓	✓
Values continuum	64		✓		✓	✓
What's in the bag?	28	✓				✓
What do I already know?	32	✓			✓	✓
Written work	54			✓	✓	✓

Baseline/Needs assessment/ Assessment for learning

A1 Draw and write

Draw and write is a well-established method used for baseline assessment. It is normally done with younger children although it does work well with older children, particularly more vulnerable young people. An example of a draw and write activity is shown here related to puberty.

This activity focuses on assessing knowledge of the emotional and physical changes that take place during puberty. The activity could be done as a baseline assessment prior to a unit on puberty. For example, a Year 7 SRE teacher may want to assess how much pupils have learnt and or remembered from primary school SRE. The drawings could then be analysed prior to the next lesson and used to inform planning. For example, if the drawings show that knowledge is good, then teaching in Year 7 could focus on issues involved in managing puberty, such as coping with wet dreams, spots or periods. If knowledge is patchy or better for girls' changes than boys' then lesson planning can be amended accordingly.

Time
20–40 minutes

Equipment
Copies of Body outline or large paper for children/young people to draw round one of their peers
Paper
Felt pens or pencils

Method
1. For a baseline assessment of the group's needs children and young people could work either on their own or in small groups. Working in single gender groups may provide interesting information on different knowledge levels of boys and girls.
2. Ask participants to draw a picture of a body, draw round a group member or give out copies of the body outline.
3. Ask them to draw and label the different emotional and physical changes that take place during puberty.
4. If the group are finding this difficult then ask them to think about:
   - heart, mind and feelings
   - skin and hair
   - sex organs
   - voice
   - good things about growing up
   - bad things about growing up.
5. Take away the pictures to plan lessons that will address any misunderstandings or gaps in knowledge and understanding. Return to these at the end of the unit – can the children/young people add to and make changes to their drawings as a result of the input?
6. Make a display to show the work that pupils have been doing.

Other draw and write topics could include, for example asking the children and young people to draw and write what they understand about what is meant by family, keeping safe or keeping clean.

Body outline

A2 What's in the bag?

This activity can be adapted and used in a variety of ways. It is a good method for engaging children and young people and can be used to assess baseline knowledge by asking children and young people what they know about a particular object or for exploring attitudes at the beginning of a unit.

Time
20–40 minutes

Equipment
A range of objects related to a particular topic and age appropriate to the year group. For example:

Hygiene: tissues, soap, deodorant, toothpaste, aftershave, perfume, washing powder, sponge, flannel, towel.

Puberty: soap, bra, tampon, sanitary towel, razor, cricket box, make-up, deodorant, shampoo, teen magazine problem page.

Relationships: mobile phone, teen magazine, *Nuts* magazine, valentine card, condom, wedding ring, baby photo, internet advert, clothes advert, make-up, World Aids Day Ribbon.

Method

1. Collect a variety of objects in a bag that will stimulate age-appropriate discussion related to the subject being covered.

2. Have children/young people seated in a circle. Explain to them that in the bag there are a number of objects that have something to do with the topic they are going to be studying.

3. Divide the group into pairs and ask one from each pair to put their hand in the bag and to select an object without looking in the bag. Once each pair has an object a variety of issues could be discussed:

   • what the object is

   • what could it have to do with the topic being studied

   • who might use it, where and how

   • what risks/benefits could there be.

4. Ask each pair in turn to introduce their object and ideas. You will need to either keep notes on the discussion or ask a child/young person to do this. The information provided by the students can then inform future planning. For example, if the group has a limited understanding of tampons and sanitary towels then more detailed work on this may have to be included in lessons on puberty or if ability to challenge stereotypes is limited (through discussion of magazine pictures for example) then this could be focused on.

A3 Graffiti sheets

This technique enables the group leader to assess levels of understanding and knowledge, and attitudes. The first example describes a needs assessment activity for HIV/AIDs, but this technique could be used for other topics, such as pregnancy options, contraceptive methods, puberty, etc. There are a number of methods that can be applied to this activity.

Time
10–15 minutes

Equipment
Large felt pens
Large sheets of paper – A2 size

Method 1

1. Working in small groups, give each group two sheets of flip chart paper, one with HIV and the other with AIDS written on it. Give students a pen each or between a pair to write down anything they know/have heard/ feel about HIV and AIDS.

2. After 10 minutes pass the sheets of paper round so that each group now has a different sheet. Explain that the task is to discuss what is written on the sheet as a group and label the statements according to:

   - things that they believe are true (✓)

   - things that they believe are untrue (✗)

   - things they are uncertain about (?).

After 10 to 15 minutes ask each group to take it in turns to feed back one statement from their sheet. Invite the other groups to challenge or offer new information. At this stage, the group leader should avoid giving too much information or correcting all misinformation. Explain to students that subsequent lessons will provide further information and opportunities to explore attitudes. For example a quiz could be designed that links directly with the group's feedback.

Method 2

1. Prepare a number of graffiti sheets, each with a statement or question on the top of them. These may be exploring views about an issue in order to assess children's and young people's understanding prior to planning a specific piece of work; or may inform what knowledge and understanding needs to be taught.

2. Display the sheets around the room so they can be written on.

3. Ask everyone to move around the room and write or draw their responses to the statements on the sheets of paper. Explain that they can write whatever they like and that there is no right and wrong answer.

Variations

Lack of space, or children and young people with mobility problems
Divide into small groups with paper and pens. Read out the statements and ask the group to write their responses, either individually or collectively, after discussing the statement. This is particularly suitable in a limited space or when working with children and young people with mobility problems.

For individual child or young person
A graffiti sheet may be developed over time when working with individuals. At the end of each session ask them to identify a key learning point from the session, what they liked about it and anything they will change as a result of the work. This may be kept by the child or young person, or by you, as a record of their progress over time.

For session in IT suite or similar
Pairs or small groups could prepare their own 'graffiti sheet' using social media or PowerPoint – these can be shared and commented on, or collated as one presentation.

Some example questions prior to work on feelings

- How do you know when you are happy?
- How do you know you are feeling confident?
- How do you feel?
- What do you think?
- Who can you ask for help if you are frightened or sad?
- Describe what it is like when you feel excited.
- How do feelings affect your behaviour?

Some example questions prior to work on sexually transmitted infections

- Can you name any sexually transmitted infections that cannot be cured?
- Where can you get a check-up for STIs?
- Can you get more than one STI at a time?
- How do condoms protect you against getting an STI?
- Why doesn't the pill protect you against STIs?

Some example questions prior to work on media, body image and pornography

- How much do magazines represent real people's lives?
- How much advertising is sexist?
- What body shapes and sizes should be used for modelling?
- What effect does airbrushing have?
- What effect would it have if magazines were forced to show models of different body sizes by law?
- What do you think about padded bras and thongs being marketed for 8-year-old girls?
- What do you think about playboy 'bunny' being used on stationery for children?
- How many people do you think have 'hang-ups' about their body and appearance?
- Why do many young people feel so unhappy about their bodies and appearance?
- What effect do the media have on young people and how they feel about their bodies?
- What could parents and carers do to encourage positive body image and self-confidence?
- What could schools do to encourage positive body image and self-confidence?
- What expectations are there of men and women to look good? And is it equal?

(Adapted from Dean and Garling, 2010)

A4 What do I already know?

Teachers in schools may be familiar with this type of process, which asks children and young people to identify what they already know about a given topic, what their thinking is and any questions they would like to have answered.

Time
10–15 minutes

Equipment
What do I already know? Grid for groups or individuals
Pens/pencils (or online version of grid if children/young people have access to computers)

Method

1. Explain what the focus of the new topic is and that you would like to find out more about what the group already knows and what more they would like to find out.

2. Give the grids out to pairs, groups or individuals to complete with some ideas about the types of things that could go into the grid. This may also relate back to some former learning that the group should have participated in.

3. Collect them in and use them to inform planning.

4. At the end of the unit give them back out for group members to check they have had their questions answered and to enable them to comment on how much they have learned as a result of the unit of work.

Example grids to be amended according to the topic/content:

What I already know about condoms	What I think about condoms	The questions I would like to ask about condoms
For example: *They stop you getting pregnant* *They can go out of date*	For example: *They are embarrassing to ask for* *They are against my religion* *They are safe*	For example: *Why are there flavoured ones?* *Do they spoil the enjoyment of sex?*

The skills I already use well in my relationships are ...	What I think about the relationship skills other people who are close to me have ...	The relationship skills I would like more help to develop are ...
For example: *Listening* *Putting my point of view across*	For example: *My closest friends are good listeners* *My mum only has time for my younger brother*	For example: *Saying no to my friends when I don't want to do something* *Sticking up for others*

A5 Carousel interview

This activity can be used to develop and peer assess skill development. It can be used to assess skills related to many themes. For example: Saying 'no' to a friend, Negotiating condom use, Practising asking someone out, etc. As with all assessment, pupils need to know what the success criteria for the activity will be, e.g. evidence of using assertiveness skills, rather than becoming aggressive. The activity requires some preparation but is worthwhile as it provides young people with the opportunity to role-play challenging situations face-to-face.

Time
20–30 minutes

Equipment
Cards with pre-prepared statements written on them – optional
Room prepared in carousel (see below)

Method

1. Prepare two circles of chairs, each with the same number of chairs. The inner circle of chairs should face outwards. The outer circle should face inwards with one chair opposite each chair in the inner circle.

2. Ask the children and young people to sit on the chairs.

3. Give each of those sitting in the inner circle a card with a statement written on it (either an excuse for not using a condom, or a friend asking you to do something you don't want to do for example). Those sitting in the inner circle read what is on the card and the outer circle have to respond using skills or knowledge they have learned in the lesson. A minute is given and then the outer circle move around to the left and are asked to respond to a different scenario, e.g. a different excuse for not using a condom.

4. When you have repeated this three or four times, ask the inner circle to feed back the best responses that they have heard.

5. Ask everyone to stand up and swap places with the person opposite them, then those on the outside move one to the right.

6. Repeat the question and answer process. Repeat the activity and ask for feedback again. The second feedback should elicit some good examples of assertiveness/negotiation skills which can be drawn out and recorded on the board. Pupils can then be asked to assess using the traffic light colour system (see page 87) how confident they are using these skills. If pupils remain under-confident further opportunities will be needed to develop and practise the skills.

7. To assess individual skills you would need to ask children and young people to either peer assess their partner, perhaps using a checklist based on the success criteria/learning outcomes, or to provide a written response to a scenario.

Layout of chairs

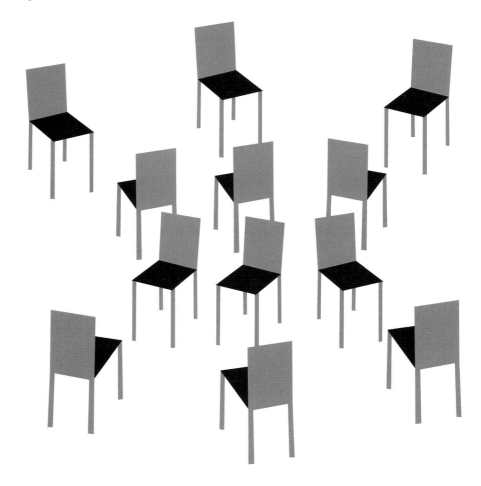

Suggested scenarios for cards to assess saying 'No' to a friend (assertiveness skills)
The outer circle are asked to find an effective way to say 'no', even if they would be agreeable to the suggestion being made.

Ask your friend:

- to come with you to your granny's house
- to steal you a Mars Bar from the corner shop
- if you can copy their homework
- if you can borrow their new top
- to come with you to meet someone you've met on Facebook
- to ask someone out for you
- to get some alcohol from their mum's house
- to pick on someone you don't like
- to come on holiday with you.

Example assessment criteria

Learning objective

- To express their views confidently (PSHE End of Key Stage 2 Statement)

Intended learning outcomes

- Working towards: I can say no to a friend.
- Working at: I can say no assertively to a friend, in a way that takes into account their feelings.
- Working beyond: I can say no to things I don't want to do in a range of situations.

Example condom excuses (ideally pupils generate these)
The outer circle are asked to find an effective way to encourage their prospective partner to use a condom or to refuse to have sex without a condom. Excuses can be written on cards.

- I'm on the pill so we don't need to use one.
- I've got a piercing, it will burst the condom.
- It spoils the moment.
- It doesn't feel as good.
- I had a chlamydia test last week and I'm clear.
- You would if you loved me.
- I've never had sex before so I haven't got an STI.
- We've done it loads of times before without a condom.

Example assessment criteria

Learning objective

- To recognise that risk assessment and management are part of life and give examples of how to manage and reduce risk in different circumstances. (PSHE: Personal Wellbeing End of Key Stage 4 Statement)

Intended learning outcomes

- Working towards: I can use simple negotiation skills when dealing with people I am close to and know well.
- Working at: I can use negotiation skills when dealing with people I am close to and know well, as well as with some people I don't know very well yet.
- Working beyond: I can use lots of different negotiation skills when dealing with people in all sorts of different situations and relationships.

(PSHE Association, 2010)

A6 Sentence stems

This activity provides feedback on what children and young people have learnt and is a useful way of finding out what else they need to learn.

It also provides an opportunity to acknowledge the successes and achievements of the group.

Time
Approximately one minute per person.

The time is dependent on the size of the group. It is important that the activity does not feel rushed and the group has the skills to listen to all group members.

Method

1. Bring everyone together in a circle.

2. Choose a suitable sentence stem (see the example sentence stems below).

3. Invite someone to start then, from the starter's left side, carry on around the circle. Each person should be encouraged to contribute.

4. Participants have the option to 'Pass' if they wish, but once the round has been completed, offer another chance to contribute.

Example sentence stems

- What I have learnt from today is ...
- I have learnt to ...
- What I need to do next is ...
- I now understand ...
- Something I will change after today is ...

These sentences can also be combined. For example, What I found out about was ... and what I shall do next is ...

A7 The story so far

This activity provides a quick and useful means of assessing levels of understanding during a session on a given topic and can help to summarise and confirm the learning so far and ensure that the learning needs of different children and young people are met. The responses from the children and young people can be used to inform planning and identify if any additional input is needed for some participants.

Time
5–10 minutes

Equipment
None

Method

1. Stop at a relevant point in the work you are doing. Then ask the children and young people, as individuals or small groups, to summarise 'the story so far' – that is, what they have learnt about and what they have learnt to do.

2. Use questions to prompt them in this – some example questions are provided below.

3. Reflect back on what the children and young people say, clarify any misconceptions and identify future learning needs.

Example questions

- What can you remember about keeping yourself safe? What is the most important thing to do?
- We have been learning about bullying and prejudice. What new things did you learn? What was important? What will you remember? What should we learn next?
- We have been learning about contraception and sexual health. Imagine a new person has just walked into the room – who can give them the story so far in 2 minutes/5 sentences? What else do we still have to learn?

A8 Self-assessment

Children and young people should be routinely encouraged to reflect on the progress they have made in sessions/lessons and across a unit of work. To do this they will need to know what it is they are working towards and be provided with tools and opportunities to explore the progress they have made and what they have achieved. There are a variety of methods for doing this. The use of traffic lights (see page 88) and fist open/closed (see case study on page 17) are techniques regularly used to gauge understanding and be used before and after an activity to assess learning. The worker can then ascertain children and young people who need additional support or input.

Continuums can also be used as a quick method of ascertaining the understanding of the group. For example, one end of the continuum could be very confident and the other end not confident at all. The worker could read out a range of skills and children and young people could be asked to place themselves on the continuum and perhaps reflect on what they might need to do to improve that skill. This would need to be handled sensitively to enable children and young people to admit skills they were less confident in.

What follows is an example using a self-assessment sheet. Self-assessment is a useful tool, but should not be the only assessment tool used.

Time
10 minutes

Equipment
Self-assessment sheet, (or online version if young people have access to computers), one per child/young person

Method

1. At the end of a session or unit of work hand out a self-assessment sheet and ask the children and young people to reflect on the knowledge and understanding and skills they have. More able and older children and young people can be asked to provide evidence of why they have assessed themselves as they have and to identify next steps.

2. If the learning environment is safe enough the children and young people can be asked to talk with a partner about their self-assessment and seek their views on it.

Self-assessment SRE Year 1 and 2

Colour a face to show how well you can do each thing. In the comments box, describe something you have got better at this term, or something you remember from your lessons.

I can list two types of families.	☹ No	☺ Yes
I can label the outside parts of the body.	☹ No	☺ Yes
I know who I can talk to if I am feeling worried about anything.	☹ No	☺ Yes
I can say four ways my body has changed since I was a baby.	☹ No	☺ Yes
I can say three things I do to keep clean and healthy	☹ No	☺ Yes

My comments:

Teacher comments:

A9 Peer assessment

In order for a child or young person to assess their peers they will need to have good communication and feedback skills and will need to be absolutely clear about what they are looking for in the work of their peers. The following is an example of a peer assessment activity related to condom skills developed by the Brighton & Hove Healthy Schools Team.

Time
30 minutes

Equipment
Condom skills checklist – one per group of three
Condom demonstrators – one per group of three
Condoms – one per young person

Method

1. The activity would follow on from a condom demonstration. Give each group of three a demonstrator, a condom each, and one condom skills grid between three. Young people take it in turns to put a condom on the demonstrator and to talk through the process. The observing young people take it in turns to assess each other by ticking the grid. Points for development are then taken back in.

2. Results from the checklist could then be recorded with those scoring full marks working beyond the End of Key Stage 3 Statement for PSHE: personal wellbeing, those scoring eight or more working at the level and those with less than eight working towards it.

Condom skills tick chart

Skill	Name	Name	Name
Able to provide a reason for using a condom			
Checked packet is undamaged			
Checked Kitemark			
Checked date			
Opened packet correctly			
Checked which way to put condom on			
Put condom on the right way round/or threw condom away			
Held teat to remove air as condom was put on			
Held condom on, rolled off			
Put in tissue and threw in bin			
Totals (out of 10)			

A10 Diamond fours/nines

This activity can be used to assess understanding of the issues, as well as develop communication and reasoning skills. Diamond fours is a simpler version to be used with younger children or those with special educational needs. Decide which version is most appropriate for your group. The statements can be generated by you or can arise from the results of a 'brainstorm' with the group. Having completed individual diamonds children and young people can be asked to self-assess or peer assess the results against learning outcomes/success criteria. Children and young people could then use this activity to lead into a summative assessment – perhaps a written task or role-play which they could work on independently.

Time
30 minutes

Equipment
An envelope for each participant – within each envelope, a set of nine (or four) diamond-shaped pieces of paper with a statement written on each.

Method

1. Explain to the children and young people that the exercise is to help them think about an issue that they have been discussing.

2. Explain that they should place the statement they think is most important, or the statement they agree with most, at the top. The statement they least agree with, or that they think is least important, should be placed at the bottom.

3. Demonstrate how it works by drawing this on a board or piece of flip chart paper.

4. After each child or young person has completed their diamond, ask them to review their responses against the learning outcomes and to peer-assess a partner. The group can then be encouraged to discuss the differences, similarities and reasons for their choices with a partner or another pair. A shared, negotiated diamond may arise.

For Diamond 4s, the pattern will have the:

- most important statement at the top
- next two most important statements side by side
- least important statement at the bottom.

For Diamond 9s, the pattern will have the:

- most important statement at the top
- next two most important statements side by side
- next three most important statements side by side
- second and third least important statements side by side
- least important statement at the bottom.

Diamond 4 template

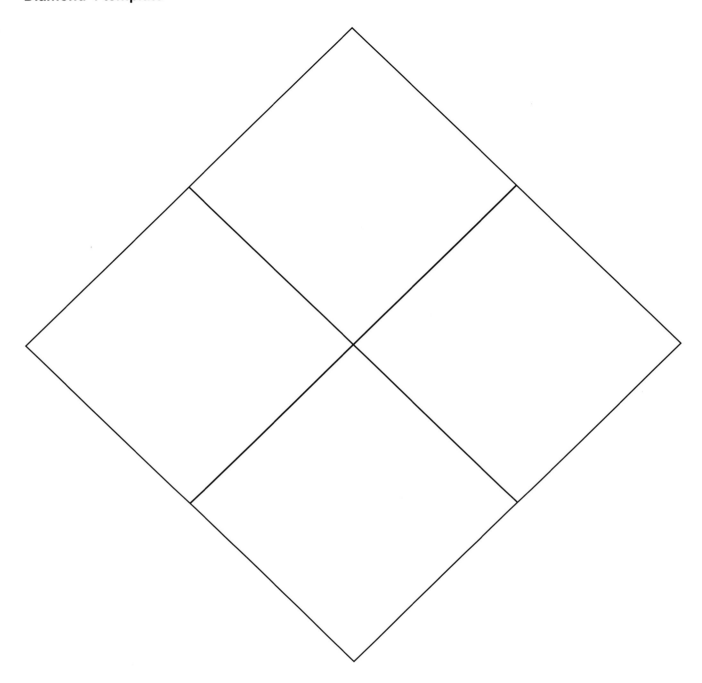

Diamond 9 template

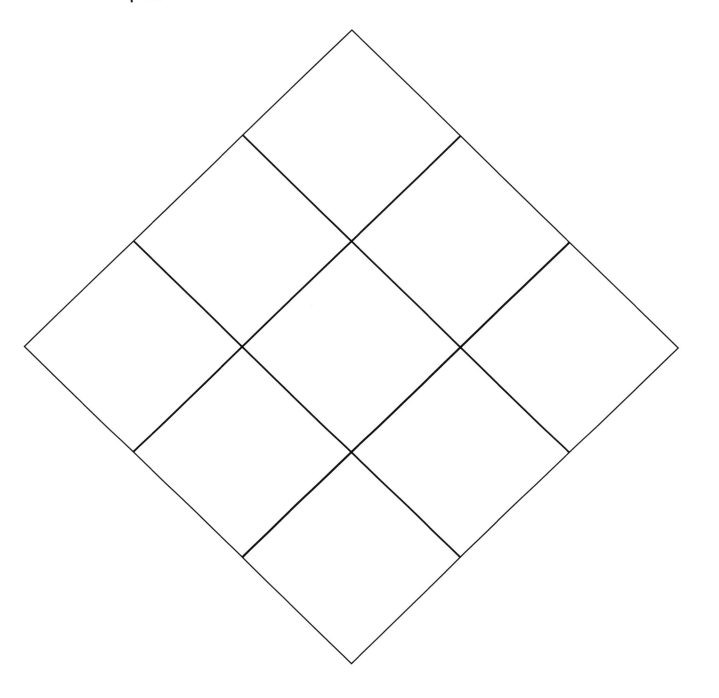

Examples of statements

When you get scared ...

- you should keep it to yourself
- tell someone and ask for help
- you should run away and hide
- you should try to stay calm.

A friend is someone ...

- who will stick up for someone else
- who tells them the truth
- who makes them laugh
- who listens to what they say
- to share things with
- who has lots of good ideas
- who wears great clothes
- who is the same age as them
- who they can trust and respect.

The best way of keeping safe is by ...

- asking for help from friends and family
- being able to say 'no' confidently
- always being home on time
- telling others where I am going and when I expect to arrive
- never keeping secrets
- not being afraid to shout out loud if necessary
- knowing how to contact the police or an ambulance
- working out the risks I might be taking beforehand
- making a quick phone call or sending a text to say I am safe.

A11 My toolbox

This activity provides a creative way of helping children and young people to reflect on the new skills they have learnt or developed. It is a useful activity when working with children and young people who do not enjoy writing, and for clarifying the skills that have been developed over a unit of work or project.

Time
10–15 minutes

Equipment
Copies of My toolbox
Pens or pencils

Method

1. Give individuals or each pair a copy of the My toolbox sheet.

2. As a group, brainstorm the range of skills that have been developed. Ask each person or pair to draw and/or write about the skills they have learnt. They can show how confident they feel about their ability to use these skills by placing them near the toolbox (inside the circle) to show they feel confident, or away from the toolbox (outside the circle) to show they are less confident. The teacher/group facilitator may want to provide a handout/whiteboard slide that lists the skills that the programme has aimed to develop for children and young people to check/add to their picture.

3. Either collect in the toolbox to inform future planning or report writing on personal development, or ask them to work in pairs and use this to identify future learning needs.

Example skills taken from the End of Key Stage Statements:

KS1
- identify and name feelings
- cooperate with others
- make simple choices

KS2
- express their views confidently
- make judgements and decisions
- show ways of maintaining good relationships
- challenge stereotyping

KS3
- manage strong emotions positively
- make informed choices

KS4
- manage and reduce risk
- challenge offensive or abusive behaviour

My toolbox

I am not confident about using these skills

I am confident
about using
these skills

Summative assessment/ Assessment of learning

A12 Advising others

This activity is a useful way of assessing learning on a particular theme by encouraging children and young people to advise someone else.

Time
20 minutes

Equipment
Paper
Pens

Method

1. Scenarios could be given to individuals, pairs or small groups. Children/ young people needing support could be given word banks or sentence stems to help them complete the task.

2. Devise a scenario, which will assess pupil knowledge of a particular issue, their skills in knowing how to give or deliver advice or their ability to explore attitudes and values. Ensure that the learning outcome for the activity identifies the skills being assessed. These learning outcomes could be differentiated, e.g. all, most, some. Explore with the pupils what the success criteria will be so that they are fully aware of what they need to do to achieve the task.

3. The children and young people can record their work either as a letter, email, text or, if they are reporting a conversation for example, using speech bubbles.

4. These can be self, peer or teacher assessed and then be kept in the personal portfolio or evidence of learning.

Example scenarios

- You are an agony aunt on a teen magazine. Sarah writes to you saying she is 11 and is very worried about her period starting. What advice do you give her?
- Your friend Ahmed is smaller than most other boys in your year. This is making him feel miserable, particularly because he is being teased and called names by a group of girls. What do you do to help him?
- A group of parents and carers who run a helpline have asked you to advise them on how they should talk to young people about sex. Write a Top Tips information sheet for them.
- A friend asks you via a private message on Facebook what the symptoms are for a sexually transmitted infection. What would you say?
- You are a peer mediator. You are told by a girl in Year 8 that she is being harassed by a group of boys in Year 9. What advice do you give her?
- You are a peer educator. You are planning a session on condom use to deliver to a group of 14 year olds in a youth club. Prepare a handout with the steps for using condoms.

Example assessment criteria for the scenario: Your friend Ahmed is smaller than most other boys in your year. This is making him feel miserable, particularly because he is being teased and called names by a group of girls. What do you do to help him?

Learning objective

- To be able to describe what bullying and stereotyping is and express ways of responding to it (PSHE: End of Key Stage 2 Statement)

Intended learning outcomes

- Working towards: I can describe what bullying is in simple terms and I can think of one way I could support someone who is being bullied.
- Working at: I can explain what bullying and stereotyping is and can think of two ways of supporting someone who is being bullied.
- Working beyond: I can explain what bullying and gender stereotyping is and can provide a range of ideas for how someone being bullied can be supported.

You don't want to write an essay, you can just do it through role-play.
Young man, aged 14

Doing plays and games helps me remember it.
Girl, aged 11

A13 Role-play

Role-play is particularly helpful for assessing the development of skills, the ability to communicate and engage with others, and for discussing different values and beliefs. The challenge is to be able to assess the individual skills of participants and to record the evidence of learning.

Time
20–30 minutes

Equipment
A scenario for each group, written on separate pieces of paper (see the examples of scenarios opposite)

Method

1. Divide everyone into large or small groups and ask each group to take a scenario out of a hat or allocate the scenarios yourself. Explain to them that each group will do the role-play, while others will watch them and assess their role-play against the learning outcomes/success criteria for the activity.

2. Provide a set amount of time to plan the role-play.

3. Explain that the peers who are watching will be giving feedback on the role-play. Remind them how to give constructive feedback. This process can be supported by providing the peer assessors with a checklist that will help them to decide how well the group have provided evidence of their knowledge, understanding and skills. It would also be helpful for the groups being assessed to have this information so they know what they are being assessed on.

4. Ask each group in turn to perform their role-play. This could be recorded using a video camera to use for reflection to aid both the learner and facilitator in assessment/self-assessment.

5. You and/or peers provide feedback on the content of the role-play and skills shown. This can then be recorded.

6. To provide information on individual achievement the role-play may need to be followed up by individual oral or written reflection on the activity.

Examples of scenarios

For small groups:

- One person has had an argument with their best friend. You are a group of friends and you are trying to help them resolve the conflict.

- One of your friends is teasing a girl in your class who has started her period. As a group of friends, what would you do?

- Your carers have said you cannot go to a birthday party that you really want to go to. How do your friends help you?

- You think you have an STI. You ask a friend to help you find out about a genito-urinary medicine (GUM) service and to come with you to the clinic.

- You have started a relationship. Your partner is from a different culture and your parents and your sister are giving you a hard time. How would you assert your views and opinions?

For larger groups:

- A young woman is pregnant. She wants an abortion and the young man wants to keep the baby. Parents/carers of the young woman support one view or the other (ask the group to choose which one). What can they do?

- A group of friends are in a youth club discussing two gay men kissing in the street. One person is homophobic, and some are supportive. What should they do?

- Some friends are in the park. One friend thinks that they may have an STI but does not know who from, and does not know where to go for help. One of the others thinks that their friend was stupid not using protection, another thinks it will go away on its own. What should they do?

Example assessment criteria for the scenario: A group of friends are in a youth club discussing two gay men kissing in the street. One person is homophobic, and some are supportive. What should they do?

Learning objective

To understand that all forms of prejudice must be challenged at every level in our lives.

Intended learning outcomes

- Working towards: I would know what to say, or who to tell, if I saw someone being treated unfairly, or if I found someone else's behaviour upsetting or offensive.

- Working at: I can challenge offensive behaviour, prejudice and discrimination in a number of appropriate ways and I can do so confidently, without becoming aggressive, or putting myself in danger.

- Working beyond: I can weigh-up the effectiveness of a range of appropriate ways to challenge offensive behaviour, prejudice and discrimination and can do so confidently, without becoming aggressive, or putting myself in danger.

(PSHE Association, 2010)

A14 Written work

With its focus on active learning and the practice and development of skills, written work is not necessarily a feature in all SRE sessions. However, it does have a role in providing evidence of individual learning and progress and if used creatively can engage children and young people and provide an opportunity to celebrate learning and achievement. Children and young people can be provided with a range of options in terms of how to present their work and tasks can be differentiated according to need with support sheets, examples and frameworks provided for the less able.

The range of written tasks that children and young people can be given include: letters, emails, texts, songs, raps, newspaper article/headline, commercials, poems, posters, leaflets, instruction manuals, PowerPoint presentations, scenes from a film/soap opera, etc. What is important is to use a range of written tasks, rather than for example writing a leaflet for each topic and where possible to give the task a purpose or meaning. For example leaflets about puberty could be sent to a Year 6 class in a local primary, a song or rap could be performed in assembly as part of peer education, campaigning emails (for example asking for more services for young people) could be sent to the local MP.

Children and young people will also need to know what the learning outcomes and success criteria are for their piece of written work. The written work could be peer assessed and/or teacher/group worker assessed, but in all cases the marking/feedback should include a formative comment that provides guidance on how to develop and improve. See the example of a written assessment on the following pages with the marking sheets and criteria.

Examples of topics

- commercial for a new brand of good friend
- commercial/advert for the local young people's sexual health service
- song about good communication
- commercial about managing menstruation
- a ditty about using condoms
- a poem about choices and peer pressure
- a commercial for soap that eradicates prejudice and stigma
- a story about falling in love
- a poem about feeling different
- a song about ending a relationship
- poster about fathers/dads
- poster about safer sex
- instruction manual about how to negotiate effectively
- leaflet on how to ask for help and advice
- leaflet about how to talk about sex with a partner
- instruction manual about how to challenge bullying
- leaflet about the importance of expressing feelings
- instruction manual about managing wet dreams/periods
- presentation on the symptoms of chlamydia and how to get tested
- presentation on what I do to feel good about myself.

Written assessment example

This assessment is taken from the East Sussex PSHE and Healthy School's Team LoveLife resource. It has been designed to be used with students in Key Stage 4. This assessment models the process involved in effective assessment.

In this assessment, you will need to explore a given scenario with students in order to show your understanding of how risky situations can offer knowledge about contraception and sexual health, as well as be able to show skills in offering support and advice to young people.

Objectives
- To demonstrate confidence in finding professional health advice and help others to do so.
- To describe the short and long-term consequences of personal health choices related to sexual activity and make decisions based on this knowledge.
  (PSHE: Personal Wellbeing End of Key Stage 4 Statements)

Method

1. Explain to the young people that they are to work in pairs or threes for this assessment using the following two scenarios:

   - Sarah is 15 and worried she might be pregnant. She had sex at a party two days ago when she was a bit drunk and wishes she hadn't. Her friend, Amy, takes her to see the school nurse.
   - Joe is 15. He has just started seeing a girl and wants to have sex with her. He goes to the young people's clinic to get free condoms.

2. Ask the young people to write a script of the scenarios giving the dialogue between:

   - the school nurse and Sarah
   - Joe and the advisor at the clinic.

3. Using the checklist on page 56, mark the scripts. This could be done by peers within the classroom.

4. See how well the young people have met the objectives and give feedback.

Criteria for success

In order to reach Level 6 or Grade (put in school marking grade) or Wt
They can describe some of the short-term and long-term consequences of personal health choices, e.g. having unprotected sex, readiness for sex and/or impact of alcohol on decision-making. They can make a decision based on this knowledge. They can assess some of the risks and benefits associated with these lifestyle choices and can make safer choices based on their assessment. They have a good knowledge of some of the contraception that is on offer as well as professional health advice and are confident in offering it. They can deliver messages around thinking about whether you are ready for sex and positive self-esteem.

In order to reach Level 7 or Grade (put in school marking grade) or Wa
They can describe many of the short-term and long-term consequences of personal health choices, e.g. having unprotected sex, readiness for sex and/or impact of alcohol on decision-making. They can weigh up other people's views as well as their own and assess the implications of this situation based on this knowledge. They can explore in detail some of the risks and benefits associated with these lifestyle choices and can offer a variety of safer choices based on their assessment. They have a good knowledge of contraception, STIs, pregnancy, and the law, as well as professional health advice and are confident in offering the correct support. They demonstrate an ability to negotiate around readiness for sex and promoting positive self-esteem.

In order to reach Level 8 or Grade (put in school marking grade) or Wb
The student shows a detailed accurate knowledge of the range of contraception available to use and how to use it appropriately. They are able to analyse the situation and offer the correct contraceptive advice accordingly. The student was able to make clear connections in the scenario and could assess the risks and benefits associated with these lifestyle choices such as sexual activity and/or using alcohol and can make safer choices based on this assessment. The student is able to offer a variety of courses of action and can draw conclusions about the consequences of these. They ask challenging questions in order to explore the situation fully. They can state where to find professional health advice in a variety of locations and can analyse which is the most appropriate.

Written assessment marking

Scenario 1

Name of student

Name of assessor

Checklist

Tick under 'yes' or 'no' column if the information in each statement has been included in the script.

Statement	Yes	No
1. Did they discuss the situation at the party?		
2. Did they talk about alcohol and risk taking?		
3. Did they talk about thinking whether they were ready for sex and were they put under any pressure? Did they attempt to counteract the pressure in any way?		
4. Did they mention condoms or other forms of contraception?		
5. Did they mention emergency contraception?		
6. Did they mention pregnancy tests?		
7. Did they talk about STIs (sexually transmitted infections)?		
8. Did they mention what options would be available if pregnant?		
9. Did they talk about where to go for further help?		
10. Did they talk about contraception for the future?		

Scenario 2

Name of student

Name of assessor

Checklist

Tick under 'yes' or 'no' column if the information in each statement has been included in the script.

Statement	Yes	No
1. Did they talk about his relationship?		
2. Did they talk about being ready for sex and pressure?		
3. Did they talk about legal issues/age of consent?		
4. Did they show how to use a condom?		
5. Did they talk about what to do if the condom split/wasn't used? E.g. emergency contraception.		
6. Did they talk about STIs (sexually transmitted infections)?		

Marksheet

Name of pupil:

Assessor:

Achievement:

Level awarded using criteria above

(Wb = Working beyond, Wa = Working at, Wt = Working towards)

Effort:

E = Excellent, G = Good, N = Needs improving, P = Poor

Reason:

One thing that could be improved would be to:

A15 Draw and write

Draw and write is often used for baseline assessment, but can be used for summative assessment. This puberty draw and write activity could be used at the end of a lesson or unit to assess knowledge and understanding of puberty. If used to assess individual achievement pupils will need to know what it is they are working towards. See example below.

Time
20–40 minutes

Equipment
Copies of Body outline for each child/young person
Paper
Felt pens or pencils

Method

1. Follow the method described in Activity A1, but ask children and young people to work individually. (Some children and young people may need support, perhaps someone to scribe for them or someone who can translate from their first language and write for them.)

2. The sheets can then be collected in for the teacher to assess or handed out to other group members to be peer assessed against the learning outcomes or success criteria.

3. Celebrate and reward achievement and effort and display the work done.

Example success criteria

Learning objective

- To understand the physical and emotional changes that take place at puberty (3f PSHE: Personal Wellbeing: Programme of Study, National Curriculum 2007)

Intended learning outcomes

- Working towards: I can list two physical changes and three emotional changes at puberty.

- Working at: I can list a range of physical and emotional changes in both boys and girls.

- Working beyond: I can explain the physical and emotional changes that take place as a normal part of growing up and and explain how these can impact on our identity and self-image.

A16 Storyboards

This method can be supportive of children and young people who have lower literacy levels as they can draw a cartoon strip to reflect their understanding and skills.

Time
20–30 minutes

Equipment
Copies of an Example storyboard (page 62)
Copies of blank story boards (page 63)
Pens, pencils and erasers

Method

1. Explain that this activity is an assessment and that participants will need to show the skills that they would use in a certain situation through a cartoon strip. The scenario or scenarios chosen will relate to the work that has been done on the subject. The example on page 62 can be used to assess the development of relationship skills. Support the less able by partially completing a cartoon strip or providing a list of prompts.

2. Give out the blank storyboards/cartoon strips and explain the success criteria for the activity and what skills they will need to show in order to achieve.

3. The resulting storyboard/cartoon strips can then be teacher or peer assessed.

Example storyboard

Scenario	Step One	Step Two	Step Three
Michael wants to end his relationship with Sunita. What are the steps he should take?	Michael needs to think about when is a good time to talk to Sunita and what he wants to say.	He might practise with someone he trusts. He needs to make sure he does it as kindly as possible.	Talk to Sunita and be kind and clear. If possible, discuss how they will behave towards each other.

Blank storyboard

Scenario	
Step One	**Step Two**
Step Three	**Step Four**

A17 Values continuum

This is a good activity for assessing children's and young people's ability to express their beliefs and listen to the views of others. It is useful for working with older young people or those who are confident in working in groups. The aim is not to agree or judge a person based on their values, rather the assessment process is to enable a judgement to be made about people's ability to discuss and engage with a range of beliefs and values. It can also be used as a formative method to help identify areas for development if a lack of empathy or understanding in one area becomes apparent.

Time
30–40 minutes

Equipment
A number of value statements. (Each statement should be written on a Post-it note, be appropriate to the maturity and understanding of the group, and be relevant to the topic being explored. See the example statements on page 65.)
Large sheets of paper
Blu-tack
Felt pens

Method

1. Divide everyone into small groups of four or five.

2. Give each group a set of statements and a large sheet of paper with a line along the longest side with 'Agree' on one end and 'Disagree' on the other.

3. Ask each group to place the statements face down around the large piece of paper.

4. Explain that each person takes a statement in turn, places it on the continuum and explains why they have placed it there. Stress that the statement can be placed anywhere along the continuum; and that group members cannot criticise or put down a person for placing it where they have on the continuum.

5. The other members of the group can either influence the decision made at each turn, or wait until all the statements have been laid before entering into a debate.

6. Reflect on the process and where possible provide one-to-one feedback.

7. Once completed, to provide information on individual achievement, the activity may need to be followed up by individual oral or written reflection on the activity with reference to identified key areas, such as: self-assessment of ability to listen to others, express own view, change/moderate view.

Example statements

These statements can be amended or changed according to the needs of the group. These examples are not suitable for use with children of primary school age.

Sex, contraception and safer sex

- The law is right to ban sex under 16.
- Condoms are important to protect against sexually transmitted infections.
- Masturbation is as good as sex with another person.
- Lots of people say they have had sex when they have not.
- Alcohol and other drugs can influence the choices people make about sex.
- Men and women have an equal desire for sex.
- People lose interest in sex when they get old.
- It is okay for a woman to have sex when she is menstruating.

Gender issues

- It is weird for little boys to play with dolls.
- Girls should not ask boys to go out with them.
- Twelve-year-old girls are always more grown up than boys of the same age.
- Girls are not as strong as boys.
- Women are naturally better carers than men.
- It is okay for boys to cry.
- Gay men are not real men.
- Boys like to play fighting games more than girls.
- Women are braver than men.
- Both mothers and fathers should look after their children equally.

Sexual beliefs and attitudes

- Men and women are equally responsible for contraception.
- You can become infected with HIV if you kiss a person who is already infected.
- Many girls get very bad-tempered before a period.
- It is okay not to have sex.
- People who are physically disabled have a right to enjoy active sex lives.
- Oral sex is not proper sex.
- Abortion is a woman's right.
- The only proper purpose for sex is to bring children into the world.
- Sex and love together are better than just sex on its own.

A18 Quizzes

Short quizzes and questionnaires are a useful teaching and learning technique that can be used in a variety of active and engaging ways to reinforce and develop subject knowledge. It may on occasions be valid to use these in a more formal 'exam' type way in order to gain an insight into the range of knowledge across the class and to identify if any children and young people have particular gaps in their understanding. There is one example below related to attitudes – this would assess a child or young person's ability to express their opinions and understand that there is a range of opinions rather than a 'test' of their attitudes. If being used as an assessment in this way you may want to encourage the children and young people to revise/prepare for it whilst being really clear about the aspect of the curriculum it is covering.

Time
10–30 minutes

Equipment
Copies of the quiz (Develop your own or use one of the quizzes provided on pages 68 to 73.)
Pens or pencils

Method

1. Give out copies of the quiz. Ask the children and young people to answer the questions, either individually, in pairs or in small groups. Tell the group that a quiz is not a test, and that no one else needs to see or mark the paper.

2. Ask the children and young people to read the questions and write down their answers in the space provided. For true and false quizzes, ask them to circle their answer or write in T for true or F for false.

3. When everyone has finished, read out the correct answers (see pages 74 and 75) and ask participants to correct their own work.

4. To finish the session, bring the whole group together to discuss the answers. Answer any questions they may have, clarify information, address any inaccuracies or misunderstandings, and identify future learning needs. You could divide the children and young people into smaller groups to share answers and record areas that require further input or research.

5. Provide information about support agencies for young people at the end of the session.

Quizzes

Contraception quiz (page 68)
A useful quiz for assessing knowledge levels at the end of work on contraception.

Gender expectations quiz (page 69)
This quiz helps to assess the levels of awareness at the beginning or end of a lesson/module on gender.

Menstruation quiz (page 70)
This quiz helps to assess knowledge levels at the beginning or end of a lesson/module on menstruation.

Puberty quiz (page 71)
This quiz helps to assess the level of knowledge at the beginning or end of a lesson/module on puberty.

Sexually transmitted infections (STIs) quiz (page 72)
This quiz assesses knowledge and understanding about STIs and where to go in order to access support. It is important for the discussions to focus on the importance of recognising symptoms and seeking help, support and treatment.

Sexually transmitted infections (true or false) quiz (page 73)
This quiz is intended to introduce information on sexually transmitted infections (STIs) and to check levels of knowledge.

Answers (pages 74 and 75)

Contraception quiz

Read the following questions and write down your answers.

1. What does contraception prevent?

2. What method of contraception also protects against sexually transmitted infections?

3. How soon after unprotected sex must emergency contraception be used?

4. Where can people go for emergency contraception and advice about pregnancy and abortion?

5. Name one local sexual health service from which young people can access help and support.

Gender expectations quiz

Read the following questions and write down your answers.

1. Describe three ways men and women are expected to behave in the UK.

2. How are these expectations different across cultures and religions?

3. How do gender stereotypes affect people's self-esteem, behaviour and choices?

4. If you could, would you change these cultural expectations and gender stereotypes of men and women? If so, how?

Assessment, Evaluation and Sex & Relationships Education

Menstruation quiz

Read the following questions and write down your answers.

1. What is menstruation?

2. Do both boys and girls menstruate?

3. What do girls and young women need to do when they are menstruating?

4. Why do some people tease and bully girls and women about menstruation?

Puberty quiz

1. Read the sentences below. Decide whether each one is true or false. If you think that it is true, then circle the **T**; if you think it is false, then circle the **F**.

    a. During puberty there are physical and emotional changes.   **T**   **F**

    b. Both boys and girls go through puberty.   **T**   **F**

    c. As our bodies change, so do our feelings.   **T**   **F**

    d. Once puberty begins you smell different.   **T**   **F**

    e. Sometimes at puberty, one breast grows bigger than the other.   **T**   **F**

    f. Puberty happens because of hormones.   **T**   **F**

2. Name two changes that happen during puberty for girls:

    a.

    b.

3. Name two changes that happen during puberty for boys:

    a.

    b.

Sexually transmitted infections (STIs) quiz

Read the following questions and write down your answers.

1. How do people catch sexually transmitted infections (STIs)?

2. How can they be prevented?

3. Where can people go for help if they think they have an STI?

4. How would someone know if they had a sexually transmitted infection?

5. Who is able to get free, confidential help from a sexual health service?

6. Name one service that young people can go to for advice and support about relationships, contraception and sexual health.

Sexually transmitted infections (true or false) quiz

Read the sentences below. Decide whether each one is true or false. If you think that it is true, then circle the **T**; if you think it is false, then circle the **F**.

1. You have to have sexual intercourse to catch a sexually transmitted infection.	**T**	**F**
2. You can catch a sexually transmitted infection more than once, even when it has been treated and cured previously.	**T**	**F**
3. Sometimes the symptoms of a sexually transmitted infection go away without treatment if you wait long enough.	**T**	**F**
4. If the symptoms of a sexually transmitted infection go away by themselves then the infection is cured.	**T**	**F**
5. A condom gives good protection against sexually transmitted infections.	**T**	**F**
6. Taking the pill protects women against sexually transmitted infections.	**T**	**F**

Quiz answers

Contraception quiz

1. Pregnancy.

2. Condoms (includes female condoms).

3. Up to 72 hours after unprotected sex, but the sooner the better. In some areas young people will also have access to 'EllaOne', which can be used up to five days (120 hours) after.

4. To a GP or a sexual health service. Many schools have one-stop-shops on site that provide sexual health advice.

5. Note: Ensure you have details of local services so you are able to give information including, where possible, directions to get to the service.

Menstruation quiz

1. Menstruation is bleeding through a girl's or woman's vagina. Each month the womb prepares itself for a fertilised egg by producing a thicker lining. If the egg is not fertilised, the lining disintegrates. This is lost as blood through the cervix and the vagina, and is known as a period.

2. No, only girls menstruate.

3. The girl or woman will need to use either a sanitary towel or tampon.

   A towel is a pad that covers the vulva to catch and absorb the blood and is worn inside a girl's or young woman's knickers. A tampon is inserted inside the vagina to absorb the blood.

4. There are different reasons why people tease and bully girls and women about menstruation. Often it is because they do not understand menstruation and sometimes, particularly when girls first start menstruating, they may be perceived as different. It is never acceptable to bully or tease someone.

Puberty quiz

1.
   a. True.

   b. True.

   c. True.

   d. True.

   e. True.

   f. True.

2. Any two of the following: menstruation, growth of body hair, breast growth, body odour, body shape changes.

3. Any two of the following: voice breaks, growth of body hair, muscle development, body odour, ability to ejaculate.

Sexually transmitted infections (STIs) quiz

1. Sexually transmitted infections (STI's) can be passed from person to person through unprotected vaginal, anal or oral sex, by genital contact and through sharing sex toys.

2. Using a condom when having sex can help prevent STI's and so can having non penetrative sex.

3. They can go to a local sexual health service or genito-urinary medicine clinic.

4. STIs cannot always be recognised because some do not have signs or symptoms. Some general signs are:

   - an unusual discharge from the penis or vagina

   - a rash around the genitals

   - itchiness around the genitals

   - sores around the genitals

   - blisters and bumps around the genitals

   - pain in the genital area

   - burning sensation when peeing or having sex

   - peeing more than usual.

   However, if you think you may be at risk don't wait for signs, seek advice.

5. Everyone is able to get free, confidential advice even if they are under 16.

6. Note: It is helpful to know the names of services. Teenage pregnancy coordinators based in the primary care trust will be able to provide you with a directory of services. A directory is also available from www.fpa.org.uk

Sexually transmitted infections (true or false) quiz

1. False. All types of penetrative sex can transmit STI's but an STI can also be passed on if there is close genital contact and the virus is active on the skin or in the pubic hair (such as pubic lice) or from one person to another if sharing sex toys without washing them or changing the condom first.

2. True.

3. True. The symptoms may go away, but the infection is still present. Even without symptoms some infections can continue to harm the internal organs of the body.

4. False.

5. True.

6. False.

Evaluation activities

Evaluation activities

Evaluation is a process through which 'judgements' are made about how effectively particular teaching approaches, activities and materials meet specific objectives.

This section contains a range of example activities that can be used to evaluate an activity, a session, a lesson, a unit of work, or a year's programme. The example questions and sentence stems provided in some activities will need to be amended to suit the needs of the children and young people and the purpose of the evaluation activity.

The activities have been split into two sections; the first being A which consists of a number of activities that can be used to evaluate an activity or session in a short amount of time. Activities in section B are designed to be used to evaluate a series of sessions/unit of work and so therefore will need to be allocated more time in order that they are effective.

Supplementary evaluation activities, originally published in the first edition of this book, are available at www.ncb.org.uk/resources/publications/support-resources/assessment-evaluation-and-sex-relationships-education

Summary of Evaluation Activities

EVALUATION	Page	Activity/ Session	Unit of work	Individually	Group
Before and after	94		✓	✓	✓
Carousel	90		✓		✓
End round	81	✓		✓	✓
Evaluation sheet	98		✓	✓	✓
Faces	82	✓		✓	✓
Field of words	83	✓		✓	✓
Graffiti wall	89	✓			✓
Post-it notes	79	✓		✓	✓
Questionnaires/Review sheets	100		✓	✓	✓
Ranking statements	92		✓	✓	✓
Ten questions	96		✓	✓	✓
Traffic lights	87	✓		✓	✓
Voting	86	✓		✓	✓

Activities for the evaluation of an activity or session

These activities are all relatively quick and provide instant feedback on the activity/session being evaluated.

E1 Post-it evaluation/Snowball

Some children and young people may find it difficult to evaluate SRE publicly. This very quick method allows you to get instant feedback without individuals feeling exposed. It may be particularly useful for one-off sessions or when a group does not know each other very well.

Time
5 minutes (or more if reading the sentences around the class)

Equipment
Paper or Post-it
Pens

Method

1. Select one of the sentence stems on page 80.

2. Write the sentence stem on the board or on a piece of flip chart paper where everyone can see it.

3. Give each child or young person a piece of paper or Post-it. Ask them to complete the sentence stem. Explain to the group what will happen with their feedback (for example, it will inform planning for next lesson or planning for when the activity is repeated with another group).

4. When they have written their response, the Post-it could be put on a flip chart or the paper posted into a 'box'. Alternatively, participants can scrunch up their paper and engage in a snowball 'fight' (depending on how well you know the class and how safe this activity will be). The statements could then be read around the circle/class.

5. If you wish, you can use more than one sentence stem.

6. The responses could be written up as a record of the students' evaluations or just read through and any changes needed to the session identified.

Example sentence stems

Choose the stem that best provides the information you need. For example if the session was on a potentially challenging issue for the children/young people you may want to find out if they felt safe or comfortable in the learning environment. The sentence stems concerned with what has been learned can provide some assessment for learning, but in this context are useful to indicate whether the planning and delivery of the session enabled children/young people to learn the stated outcomes for the session.

- What went well in the session was …
- The session would have been even better if …
- I thought the activities used were …
- If you are going to do this activity again you should …
- The most interesting thing was …
- One thing I enjoyed was …
- I learned best when we ...
- I really liked ...
- I didn't like ...
- I would have liked more of ...
- The most important thing I learnt was …
- As a result of the work we have done I will change …
- Next time, I hope we will ...
- Right now I feel ...
- I felt challenged when ...
- I felt uncomfortable when ...
- I now think ...
- I have learnt to ...

E2 End round

This activity provides instant evaluation on a piece of learning. It requires the group to be able to listen to each other for the time it takes for the round to be complete. This is more suitable for a group known well to the practitioner or a group who demonstrate maturity and trust during the session.

Time
Depends on numbers in the group

Method

1. Bring everyone together in a circle.

2. Choose a suitable sentence stem (see the example sentence stems on page 37) and explain the purpose of the activity.

3. Invite someone to start then, from the starter's left side, carry on around the circle. Each person should be encouraged to complete the sentence.

4. Participants have the option to 'Pass' if they wish, but once the round has been completed, offer another chance to contribute. Some practitioners ask every participant to say the beginning of the sentence stem and then to pass. This ensures that everyone says something in the whole group.

5. After the round the group leader may want to note down any pertinent comments to inform future planning or the group could be encouraged to summarise their reactions themselves.

E3 Faces

This simple drawing activity helps to gain feedback about the learning process and to monitor the feelings in the group. Responses can be dated and used as an evaluation record. If working with individual children and young people (or providing individual support to a child in a group), particularly those who are marginalised and vulnerable, this exercise can be done at the end of each session and the Post-it notes can be dated and kept in a book or diary. As trust and cohesion develop, this 'logbook of feelings' can be used to reflect on the developmental process over time to identify how ease and confidence has grown.

Time
5 minutes

Equipment
Post-it notes or pictures of the faces for each participant
Pens
Large sheet of coloured paper on the wall or a 'feeling' logbook

Method

1. Give everyone a Post-it note and pen.

2. Explain that they are going to be asked to draw a smiley face, a sad face, a neutral face or a confused face on the Post-it note to show how they feel about the session's process or content.

3. Ask them to think about how they feel after taking part in the work and draw one of the four faces on their Post-it note to represent the feeling.

4. Ask them to stick the faces onto a large piece of paper.

5. If relevant, encourage each person to look at all the faces and to comment on what they see. Are there more happy faces? Or are they sad or confused? What does this mean about the work?

Variation for an individual child or young person
Ask the child or young person to draw or stick the face into a book or diary, known as the 'feeling logbook', and date it.

Use this feedback to gauge how emotionally safe the learning is and if individual needs are being met.

Example faces

Happy

Sad

Neutral

Confused

E4 Field of words

This quick activity gives children and young people the opportunity to express what they feel and think about a piece of work by circling any words that they feel are appropriate. There are two Field of words sheets, on pages 84 and 85. Choose the one most suitable for the group you are working with or make your own – perhaps including local slang and dialect.

Time
5 minutes

Equipment
Copies of one of the Field of words sheets
Pens

Method

1. At the end of a piece of work, give out the Field of words sheet and explain that there are a range of thoughts and feelings on the sheet.

2. Ask the children or young people to circle as many of the words as they want that reflect their thoughts and views about the work. Explain that the sheet is anonymous and you will be using it to inform future planning, so it is helpful if they provide as honest answers as possible.

   Explain that if there are no words on the sheet that represent their thoughts and feelings, they can write in new words.

3. Collect the sheets in and, if appropriate, explain when they will get their sheets returned.

Field of words (1)

What I learnt about was ...

ok   scary   boring

disappointing   embarrassing

encouraging   informative   excellent

interesting   challenging   difficult

annoying   special   inspiring

helpful   fun   concerning

a waste of time   great

funny   upsetting

stupid   alarming

I thought the methods were ...

interesting   good   OK as they are

challenging

unsuitable and need changing for next time

boring   useful   embarrassing

Field of words (2)

In this session I felt …

happy   safe   tired

angry   embarrassed confident

proud   peaceful   left out   scared

frustrated   enthusiastic

bored   naughty   alone

great   included   upset   stupid

If I was in charge I would:

E5 Voting

This activity uses hand signals to evaluate participants' views about the effectiveness of work. It gauges instant reactions and represents the immediate mood of the group. This is a particularly useful form of evaluation if the levels of literacy are low or vary considerably within the group.

Time
5–10 minutes

Equipment
A set of statements. (See the example statements below or create your own set of statements relating to the piece of work completed.) The statements need to be written in such a way as to find out the general mood of the group, how things are progressing generally and/or what everyone thinks about certain aspects of the content.

Method

1. Explain that everybody will be asked to use a range of specific hand and body signals in response to certain statements. Then show and agree upon the signals to be used (see the suggested signals below). Different groups may prefer different signals. Be aware that hand signals have cultural variations that are neutral to some and offensive to others.

2. Tell each child or young person that they should respond quickly to each statement with one of the agreed signals, without discussion and without allowing too much time to think.

3. Read out the statements.

4. Record the number of children and young people in the class and the number who agree or strongly agree. This information can then be used to inform future planning or the group could be encouraged to summarise their reactions themselves.

Suggested signals

Strongly agree Two thumbs up
Agree One thumb up
Don't know Arms folded across chest
Disagree One thumb down
Strongly disagree Two thumbs down

Suggested statements

- I got the information I wanted.
- I learned about things I didn't know before.
- I felt comfortable and relaxed.
- I need more information.
- I want to move on to a different subject.
- The information has made me feel differently or changed my mind about things.

E6 Traffic lights

This activity can be used with children and young people who either do not want to, or cannot, write. It is a very simple and quick form of evaluation. Some schools have ready-made red, amber and green cards or pages in homework diaries/journals, which are red, amber and green.

Time
5 minutes

Equipment
Copies of Traffic lights (page 88)
Red, green and yellow felt pens

Method

1. Give out the Traffic lights. Explain how the feedback will be used.

2. Explain that you are going to ask three questions. Ask them to colour in each set of traffic lights, choosing either red (the top light) to show that it was not good, they feel unhappy or they disagree; yellow (the middle light) to show that it was okay, or they are not sure; and green (the bottom light) to show that it was really good, that they are happy with the work or agree with the statement.

3. Give them a maximum of three evaluation questions. For example:

   • Did activity X help you to learn more about Y?

   • Did you feel safe to learn today?

   • Should we use this activity with another class/group?

4. If the group is using ready-made coloured cards or pages for the activity then it is important that the feedback is recorded some other way to inform planning.

Traffic lights

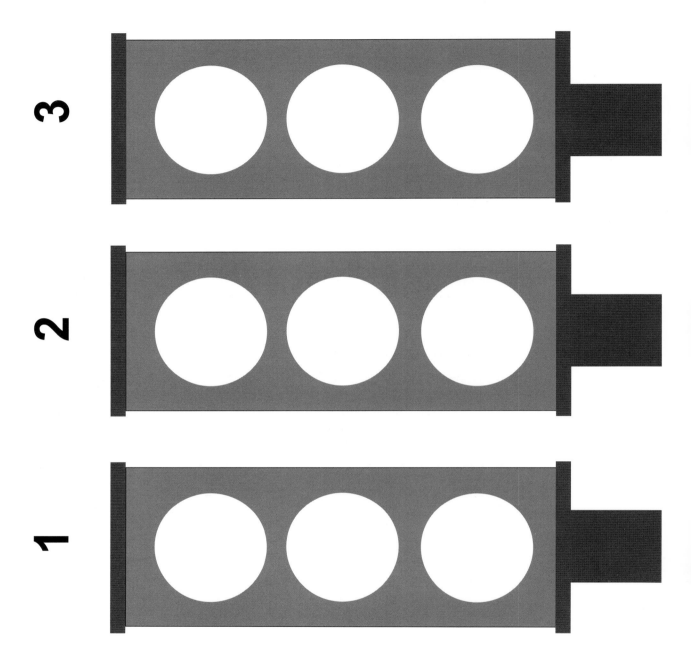

E7 Graffiti wall

This activity provides a good way of ensuring ongoing feedback throughout a project or unit of work. It also encourages reflection, makes a public record of the work, and can be used as a 'before and after' record of the process.

Time
10 minutes

Equipment
Sheets or rolls of coloured paper – or prepare a 'graffiti page' on an interactive whiteboard presentation
Several thick marker pens
String
Drawing pins
Large wall space or notice board

Method

1. Cover a large wall space or notice board with the coloured paper and attach a marker pen to each sheet of paper with the string and drawing pins or prepare a 'graffiti page' on an interactive whiteboard presentation.

2. Explain that they will be able to write and draw on the paper/whiteboard at the end of the session.

3. At the end of the session, invite the group to write or draw their comments and ideas about the work they have just completed on the graffiti wall. Ensure that you make an agreement about the language to be used when writing on the paper/board. Stress that it will be up to everyone in the group to decide what to write.

4. Agree how often the wall will be updated (which could be at the end of each session or at the end of each topic).

5. If possible, the graffiti wall can be (printed and) left up for the whole of the project, with children and young people adding regular updates. This will ensure that the information and comments remain up to date, relevant and 'owned' by the group, and will support group cohesion by providing a public record of the work they are doing together.

6. The group leader can then review the wall to review planning for the next session and at the end it can be used to celebrate the learning journey.

Example statements for graffiti wall

- What helped you to learn today?
- Something I found interesting was …
- I would still like to know more about/be able to …
- What could be done to improve this session?
- How well did the group work together/listen to each other?
- How well did the group keep to the ground rules?
- What surprised you about the session/activity?

Example activities for evaluation of a series of sessions/unit of work

E8 Carousel

This activity gives children and young people the opportunity to hear what others have learnt from the work and how effective they think it is. It can be particularly useful at the end of a unit of work as a longer evaluation session, as it can precede a written evaluation activity by encouraging children and young people to think about the process and what has been learnt before writing. It involves some room preparation but the layout provides young people with the opportunity to ask and answer questions of a range of people in a structured way.

Time
15–30 minutes

Equipment
A hall or large room with chairs prepared in circles (see method below or page 35 for illustration).
One card per pair with a question on it. (Each card should have a different question on it and the question should relate to the work just completed – see the suggested questions below and or the sentence stems on page 37.)

Method

1. Prepare two circles of chairs, each with the same number of chairs. The inner circle of chairs should face outwards. The outer circle should face inwards with one chair opposite each chair in the inner circle.

2. Ask the children and young people to sit on the chairs.

3. Give each of those sitting in the inner circle a card with a question written on it. Tell them that they will ask the question of the person who is sitting opposite them in the outer circle – this person will then have one minute to give their answer. Explain that there are different questions and that everyone will get a chance to ask and answer some questions.

4. When the minute is up, ask those in the outer circle to move around to the left and repeat the process.

5. When you have repeated this two or three times, ask everyone to stand up and swap places with the person opposite them, then those on the outside move one to the right.

6. Repeat the question and answer process.

7. Facilitate a whole group discussion to draw out key evaluation points.

Suggested questions

- What went well in this unit of work?
- What would have made the unit of work even better?
- What if anything helped you to learn today?
- Was there anything that you felt challenged by?
- How interesting and useful did you find the approach and methods?
- If you were prime minister what would you change as a result of what you have learnt?
- Having done the work, if you had to summarise what you have learnt in three bullet points, what would they be?
- If you had to describe the work we have done to someone who is a year younger than you, what would you say?
- What would you like to change about your behaviour or encourage others to change?
- If you were to do this work again, what would you do differently?

E9 Ranking statements

This activity is an opportunity to find out what everyone thinks about the work being undertaken. It gives children and young people an opportunity to explore their values and feelings, and provides feedback to you. It also promotes the development of decision-making skills. This activity could equally be carried out using an online package such as Survey Monkey[4] (or similar).

Time
10–15 minutes

Equipment
Copies of Ranking statements sheet or your own amended version to meet the needs of the group
Pens

Method

1. Explain that the exercise is to find out how everyone thinks and feels about the work so far. Tell them that honest responses are important and they can choose to make their responses anonymous.

2. Give everyone a copy of the Ranking statements sheet. Ask each child/young person to consider the statements and rank them from highest (1) to lowest (9) according to how each statement best describes their thoughts and feelings about the work so far. They can leave three statements unnumbered.

3. Acknowledge that it may be difficult to make choices but decisions have to be made. Once completed, collect the sheets in for analysis (this could then be shared with the group to discuss what might change/stay the same).

---

4 At the time of publication, this package could be found at www.surveymonkey.com.

Ranking statements

Rank these statements from highest (1) to lowest (9) according to how each statement best describes your thoughts and feelings about the unit of work. Leave three statements unnumbered.

☐ I feel satisfied.

☐ I am not learning anything new.

☐ I wish the other people would be more serious.

☐ I would like more information.

☐ This course is not interesting.

☐ This course is really great.

☐ I am being challenged.

☐ Sometimes I feel really uncomfortable.

☐ This course might be useful for some people but not for me.

☐ The information is good but the activities were rubbish.

☐ The work was good but the worker was embarrassed and uncomfortable.

☐ The way it was delivered was interesting.

E10 Before and after

This simple activity allows children and young people to record their feelings, thoughts, hopes and aspirations before a piece of work and then, afterwards to evaluate how well these have been met. It is particularly useful for reflecting on the process.

Time
5 minutes before and after a piece of work

Equipment
Copies of Before and after (page 95)
Pens

Method

1. Give each child or young person a copy of the Before and after sheet before a piece of work is carried out. Ask them to fill in the 'before' section of the form about their attitudes to the work prior to doing it. You will need to give them the topic title. For example: Puberty, Healthy Relationships, HIV.

2. Collect in the sheets and repeat the process after the activities/lessons.

3. Facilitate a brief discussion on the process and identify any future learning needs.

4. You may find it useful to collect the sheets in order to record their comments, before returning them to the children or young people so that they may keep in their personal logs/work books.

Before and after

Topic title:		
	Before learning about this topic	**After learning about this topic**
I feel …		
I think …		
I want to know/ be able to …		
The most interesting thing I learned was …		

E11 Ten questions

This activity gives children and young people the opportunity to write or verbalise with a scribe their responses to questions.

Time
20 minutes

Equipment
Copies of Ten questions – amended to suit needs of the group.
Pens or pencils

Method

1. Give each person a copy of the Ten questions sheet.

2. Explain who will see the sheet, how the information will be used and whether it will be returned to them.

3. Ask them to write their response to each question. (The activity could also be carried out as an 'interview' in pairs or groups.)

4. Collect in the sheets and analyse them to inform future planning.

Ten questions

Date:

You can draw or write in these boxes. Please provide as much detail as you can.

1. What was good?	2. What was better?
3. What was bad?	4. What was worse?
5. What was new?	6. What was the same?
7. What wasn't there?	8. What made you smile?
9. What made you sad?	10. What next?

E12 Evaluation sheet – Person outline

This is another form of evaluation that encourages children and young people to reflect in terms of thinking, feeling and actions.

Time
10 minutes

Equipment
Copies of Person outline
Pens or pencils

Method

1. Give each person or group a copy of the person outline. Structure the activity by giving examples of what could go in each section.

2. Invite some group members to feed back their actions.

3. Collect in and use to inform planning. Return to children/young people to include in learning logs/journals or similar.

Person outline

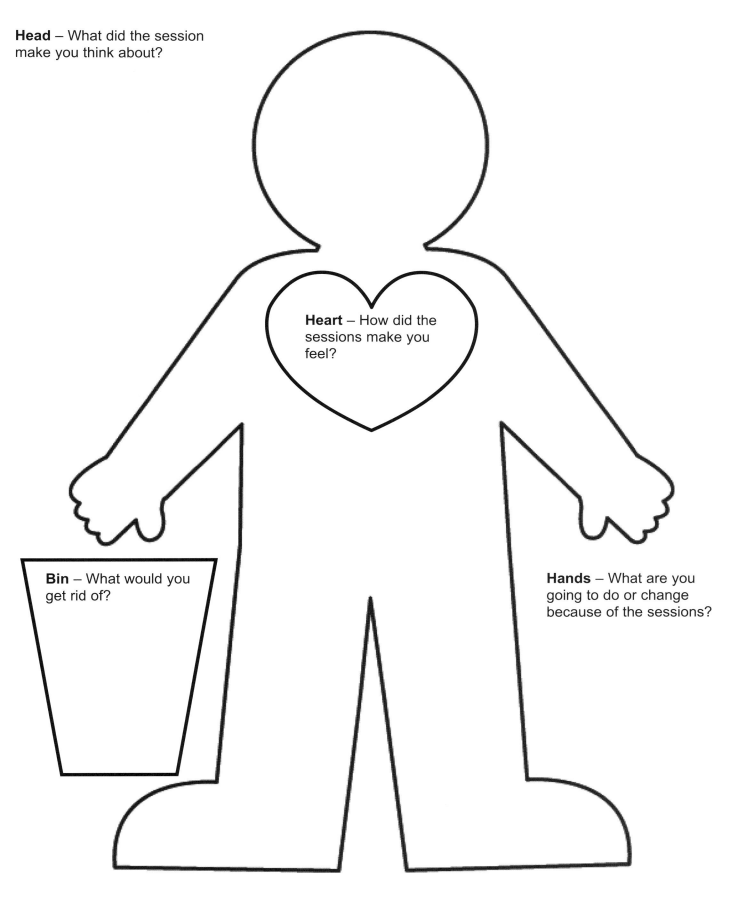

Head – What did the session make you think about?

Heart – How did the sessions make you feel?

Bin – What would you get rid of?

Hands – What are you going to do or change because of the sessions?

E13 Using questionnaires/review sheets to evaluate SRE

A questionnaire can be a powerful evaluation tool. They can provide a large sample, although feedback may not be detailed. Questionnaires could be used to inform what would be a useful purpose for a focus group. (See SEF *Are you getting it right?* toolkit (2008) for focus group activities). However, they can also be complex and time consuming to undertake. Getting the questions right can often be challenging. Asking for child/young person input into the design of questionnaires can be helpful.

There are seven stages that you need to consider if you want to successfully use questionnaires to undertake your consultation.

1. Define the purpose of your evaluation – what is it that you want to know?

2. Identify the population and sample that you wish to survey – who are you going to ask the questions of?

3. Decide how to collect the replies to your questionnaire.

4. Design your questionnaire.

5. Run a pilot study – test out the questions to see whether you are asking what you think you are asking.

6. Carry out your main survey.

7. Analyse your data.

Key points when using questionnaires:

- You need to ensure that you ask the right questions. This will depend on the purpose of the questionnaire.
- Consider when you are designing your questions how you will analyse the data you are collecting.
- Decide whether to use open or closed questions. Answers from open questions can be difficult to analyse and can take the respondent longer to answer. Closed questions can be helpful in offering the respondent a series of common answers and so make data analysis easier. However, knowing what the most likely answers are going to be can be tricky.
- Keep the layout clear and consistent. Use a bold face font for the question text and number each question. The font type should be at least 12.
- In many cases you will not want to survey all of your potential population (i.e. the whole school or a whole year group), as this would be too much work. You therefore need to define a sample, or representative group from the population.
- Reassure students about confidentiality and the purpose of the questionnaire. Collect the smallest amount of personal information that you need.
- Make the questionnaire accessible and if appropriate read out all the questions to those completing the questionnaire or provide support for individuals.
- Feed back the results of the survey to those who took part.

End of unit or end of year: Reflection/Review/Evaluation

These example questionnaires[5] or review sheets are useful for evaluating a major piece of work. It is a way of recording child/young person views about the process. These can then be used to inform follow-up focus groups and or a review of the planning. If names are collected on the sheets they can potentially be used to identify children and young people who are struggling as part of the group. This method of evaluation should be used sparingly and with a clear and specific purpose, so that children and young people engage with the process as positively as possible. The results/impact of these evaluations should be fed back to the group of young people.

Time
10–20 minutes

Equipment
Copies of the chosen questionnaire amended to meet the needs of the group and purpose of the evaluation
Pens (unless carried out online, e.g. Survey Monkey[6] package)

Method

1. Give a copy of the questionnaire to each child or young person. Inform the group whether or not the questionnaire will be confidential.

2. If they have sufficient reading and writing skills, ask them to complete it. If not, it should be read out and their answers recorded by the worker (in one-to-one settings) or a learning or support mentor (in group settings).

3. Collect in the sheets and explain how the information will be used to review and develop the unit of work for the next group. The sheets could be returned and be kept in logs or profiles.

---

5 Page 104 includes a reference to a SEAL resource. Although SEAL is no longer promoted by the Department of Education, SEAL resources are available from www.teachfind.com

6 At the time of publication, this package could be found at www.surveymonkey.com.

R1 Reflection

Reflection on unit about _____

I am …….. years old

I am a boy/girl

About the content
Did you learn anything new or interesting? If yes, what?

Did you learn any new skills? If yes, how do you think you will use them?

Do you now think differently about anything? If yes, what?

Do you think you might do anything differently? If yes, what?

What else do you need to know or think about?

Who can you ask and how will you find out?

Was anything left out?

About the process
Did you enjoy the way the class worked together?

What did you think was good?

What would you want to happen differently if you were involved in similar work again?

R2 Review sheet

Name (optional):   **Date:**

What did you learn about?

What did you learn to do?

Has the work changed your opinions in any way?   Yes/No
If yes, how?

How do you think your mind was changed?

Who or what made you change your mind?

What else do you feel you need to know/think about?

How will you find out?

How did you learn best?
(circle the relevant methods)

- by talking to my peers
- by writing about my opinions
- by visiting a local sexual health service
- by researching on the internet
- by researching in books
- by doing a quiz
- by getting answers to my questions

- by looking at leaflets
- by watching a video
- by drawing and art work
- by drama activities
- by listening to a speaker
- by discussion

Please finish the following sentences:

I learnt about

I think that

I learnt to

I was pleased when I

I enjoyed the way we learnt

I think it would have been better if

If I was doing it again I would like to

As a result of doing this work I will

Any other comments

Assessment, Evaluation and Sex & Relationships Education

R3 About my sex and relationships education (Key Stage 1 SEAL Audit)

Name: **School:**

Year Group: **Age:**

Girl ☐   **Boy** ☐   **(Please tick)**

Here are some statements about your sex and relationships education lessons. We will use your answers to help us make lessons even better. Read each sentence and then colour in the face that best describes how much you agree. Your teacher will help you if you need it.

About my school

		Yes	Don't know	No
1.	I enjoy sex and relationships education lessons at school.	☺	😐	☹
2.	I feel safe in the classroom.	☺	😐	☹
3.	I liked watching the DVD about friendships and body parts.	☺	😐	☹
4.	I liked working in groups.	☺	😐	☹
5.	I liked doing the role-play activity.	☺	😐	☹
6.	I can talk to adults in my school about things that are worrying me.	☺	😐	☹

Thank you for your help

R4 Whole-class questionnaire

We would like to ask you a few questions about your sex and relationships education (SRE) lessons. The information you provide will be used to develop the SRE programme for next year. Please answer as truthfully as possible. There are no right or wrong answers.

1. Which of the following topics have you done in SRE this year?
   [Tick as many as you like and add any that are missing.]

   ☐ Puberty ☐ Friendships & relationships ☐ Contraception ☐ Self-esteem

   ☐ STIs (sexually transmitted infections) ☐ Condoms ☐ Bullying

   ☐ _____ ☐ _____

2. Here is a list of different types of teaching and learning activities. Tick the ones that helped you to learn and put a cross by ones which did not help you to learn.
   [Add types of activities that are missing.]

   ☐ Discussion ☐ Role-plays ☐ Videos ☐ Making posters

   ☐ Quizzes ☐ Worksheets ☐ Visitors ☐ _____

3. Do you feel comfortable to speak out in PSHE lessons? [Tick one]

   ☐ Always ☐ Sometimes ☐ Hardly ever ☐ No

4. What would make you feel more comfortable in lessons?

5. Which was the best lesson you have had in SRE, and why?

6. If you could give your SRE lessons a mark out of 10 what would you give?

   ☐ 0 ☐ 1 ☐ 2 ☐ 3 ☐ 4 ☐ 5 ☐ 6 ☐ 7 ☐ 8 ☐ 9 ☐ 10

7. How would you improve the SRE lessons?

8. Which topics would you like to cover next year?

9. Do you know who you can talk to in school if you have any concerns/worries?

   ☐ Yes ☐ No

   If yes, who? _____

R5 General questionnaire

We would like to ask you a few questions about your SRE (sex and relationships education) lessons. The information you provide will be used to develop the SRE programme. Please answer as truthfully as possible. There are no right or wrong answers.

First, a little bit about you.

Are you: Male? Female? (circle)

Which year are you in? _____

Please tick one box for each question.

	Yes	No	Comment
Have you participated in different types of activities in your SRE lessons (e.g. discussions, role-play, videos, etc.)?			
Do your SRE lessons help you to feel good about yourself?			
Do your SRE lessons give you easy to understand information about sex and relationships?			
Is there a 'safe' feeling created in your SRE lessons so that people feel comfortable to talk?			
Do you know where to go to in school if you have any concerns/ worries?			
Do your SRE lessons provide you with information about where to go (outside of school) to get help and advice about sexual health?			

Useful organisations

Sex Education Forum
8 Wakley Street
London
EC1V 7QE
020 7843 1901
www.ncb.org.uk/sef

The Sex Education Forum (SEF) is the national authority on SRE. It is a collaborative network of over 90 members including local and national organisations and individuals, as well as 750 practitioners who all believe that good quality SRE is an entitlement for all children and young people. It works with its 49 member organisations to achieve this. SEF publishes a range of factsheets and publications.

Please see the website for details of SEF members who are actively involved in the development and delivery of SRE programmes.

ASDAN
Wainbrook House
Hudds Vale Road
St George
Bristol
BS5 7HY
01179 411 126
www.ASDAN.co.uk

ASDAN (Award Scheme Development and Accreditation Network) is an approved awarding body offering a number of programmes and qualifications to develop life skills, from Key Stage 3 through to adult life, from preparatory to Entry Level and on through to Key Skills Level 4.

Assessment Reform Group
The Assessment Reform Group (ARG) has been at the forefront of challenging thinking and practice in relation to all aspects of assessment, including assessment for learning. It has also worked closely with teachers, teacher organisations and local authority staff to advance understanding of the roles, purposes and impacts of assessment.
http://www.aaia.org.uk/afl/assessment-reform-group/

Department of Education
Castle View House,
East Lane,
Runcorn,
Cheshire,
WA7 2GJ
0370 000 2288
www.education.gov.uk

The Department of Education provides a non-statutory programme of study for PSHEE at Key Stages 3 and 4, and attainment target level descriptions. It also provides a website outlining the statutory information and guidance on all aspects of National Curriculum assessment and reporting for the Early Years Foundation Stage and Key Stages 1, 2 and 3.

http://www.education.gov.uk/schools/teachingandlearning/curriculum/
secondary/b00198880/pshee
http://www.education.gov.uk/schools/teachingandlearning/assessment/
a00197251/assessment-and-reporting-arrangements

Information, research and papers related to the issue of teenage pregnancy and the national efforts to reduce the rate of women aged under-18 becoming pregnant.

http://www.education.gov.uk/childrenandyoungpeople/healthandwellbeing/
teenagepregnancy

Healthy Schools
The Department for Education continues to support the Healthy Schools Programme and nationally produced materials are available on the Department for Education website: www.education.gov.uk/healthyschools To find support in your local area Google 'healthy schools' + the name of your area.

National Open College Network
The Quadrant
Parkway Business Park
99 Parkway Avenue
Sheffield
S9 4WG
0114 227 0500
www.nocn.org.uk

The National Open College Network (NOCN) is a leading UK awarding organisation, offering high quality, flexible, credit-based qualifications and is accredited by the Regulatory Authorities in England, Wales, Scotland and Northern Ireland. Open College Networks (OCNs) are licensed by NOCN. They are locally managed, not-for-profit partnerships committed to providing a flexible and responsive local accreditation service for a wide range of learning activities, including the NOCN Level 1 and 2 Award in Personal Well-Being.

PSHE Education Association
CAN Mezzanine
32–36 Loman Street
London
SE1 0EH
020 7922 7950
www.pshe-association.org.uk

The PSHE Association is the subject association for all professionals working in Personal, Social, Health and Economic education. Its mission is to raise the status, quality and impact of PSHEe, and enable high quality teaching and learning in schools.

References

Black, P and William, D. (1998) *Inside the Black Box: Raising standards through classroom assessment.* Kings College: London.

Dean, L and Garing, D (2010) *Fantasy vs Reality: the impact and influence of pornography on young people.* Brighton & Hove City Council and NHS

Ofsted (2007) *Time for Change*, London: Office for Standards in Education
Available: http://www.ofsted.gov.uk/resources/time-for-change-personal-social-and-health-education-0
Accessed 02/02/12

Ofsted (2010) *Personal, Social, Health and Economic Education in Schools.* London: Office for Standards in Education
Available: http://www.ofsted.gov.uk/resources/personal-social-health-and-economic-education-schools
Accessed 02/02/11

Ofsted (2012) *The evaluation schedule for the inspection of maintained schools and academies* London: Office for Standards in Education
Available: http://www.ofsted.gov.uk/resources/
evaluation-schedule-for-inspection-of-maintained-schools-and-academies-january-2012
Accessed 02/02/12

PSHE Association (2010) *Planning and assessing PSHE education: Assessment in Secondary PSHE education.*
Available http://www.pshe-association.org.uk/uploads/media/27/7359.pdf
Accessed 19/12/11

PSHE Association (2010) *Planning and assessing PSHE education: Personal Wellbeing Learner-Friendly Version for Key Stages 3 and 4*
Available: http://www.pshe-association.org.uk/uploads/media/27/7470.pdf
Accessed 12/01/12

PSHE Association (2010) *Planning and assessing PSHE education: Personal Wellbeing-Progression Framework for Planning & Assessment in PSHEe.*
Available: http://www.pshe-association.org.uk/uploads/media/27/7471.pdf
Accessed 30/01/12

PSHE Association (2010) *PSHE definitions: PSHE education – working definitions and relationships.*
Available http://www.pshe-association.org.uk/content.aspx?CategoryID=335&ArticleID=335
Accessed 11/01/12

Sex Education Forum (2008) *'Are you getting it right? Toolkit for consulting young people on sex and relationships education at Key Stages 3 and 4.* Available: http://ncb.org.uk/media/188096/sef_audit_toolkit_2008.pdf Accessed 11/01/12

Sex Education Forum (2011) *Survey report: young people's experiences of HIV and AIDS education.* Available: http://ncb.org.uk/media/333229/young_people_experiences_of_hiv_and_aids.pdf Accessed 11/01/12

Sex Education Forum (2012) *Values and Principles.* Available: http://www.ncb.org.uk/sef/about-us/values-and-principles Accessed 09/01/12

Further Reading

DfEE (2000) *Sex and Relationship Education Guidance*. Nottingham: Department of Education and Employment
Available: https://www.education.gov.uk/publications/standard/publicationDetail/Page1/DfES%200116%202000
Accessed 02/02/12

Ofsted (2002) *Sex and Relationships* London: Office for Standards in Education
Available: http://www.ofsted.gov.uk/resources/sex-and-relationships-education-schools
Accessed 02/02/12

Ofsted (2012) *Generic grade descriptors and supplementary subject-specific guidance for inspectors on making judgements during subject survey visits to schools*
Available: http://www.ofsted.gov.uk/resources/generic-grade-descriptors-and-supplementary-subject-specific-guidance-for-inspectors-making-judgements
Accessed 02/02/12

Sex Education Forum (2010) Understanding Sex and Relationships Education: A Sex Education Forum Briefing.
Available: http://ncb.org.uk/media/183589/understanding_sre_2010.pdf
Accessed 12/01/12

United Nations (1989) *The Convention on the Rights of the Child.* Adopted by the General Assembly of the United Nations on 20 November 1989. Geneva Defence for Children International and the United Nations Children's Fund.
Overview available: http://www.unicef.org/crc/files/Rights_overview.pdf
Accessed 12/01/12